Saml A. Rice

BRIG. GEN. SAMUEL A. RICE

Marula

An imprint of Arcadia Publishing

History of the 33rd Iowa Infantry Volunteer Regiment, 1863–6
by A.F. Sperry

A Marula Historical Reprint
Originally published in 1866

Published by Arcadia Publishing
Charleston SC

ISBN 978-0-7385-9463-7

Printed in the United States of America

For all general information contact Arcadia Publishing at:
Telephone 843-853-2070
Fax 843-853-0044
E-mail sales@arcadiapublishing.com
For customer service and orders:
Toll-Free 1-888-313-2665

Visit us on the Internet at www.arcadiapublishing.com

HISTORY

OF THE

33D IOWA INFANTRY

VOLUNTEER REGIMENT

1863–6

BY A. F. SPERRY

DES MOINES
MILLS & COMPANY 46 COURT AVENUE
1866

MILLS & COMPANY,
PRINTERS,
DES MOINES, IOWA.

o

PREFATORY.

In presenting this history of our Regiment to my fellow-soldiers of the 33d Iowa Infantry, I hope their memories while reading, may be as warm and pleasant as have been mine while writing it.

For whatever of omission or error it contains, I have only to say, that the whole was written amidst the very press of editorial and many other duties, and a very great part of it after nine o'clock at night. The work is as well as I could make it under the circumstances.

Much of monotony may be ascribed to the sameness of the events to be described; and many omissions may be accounted for by lack of data which others should have furnished, as requested, and as they promised to do.

And hoping this volume may but bring more vividly to memory, the times we have passed together in our noble old Regiment, I am,

Very Respectfully,

A. F. SPERRY.

PANORA, IOWA, April 24th, 1866.

CONTENTS.

CHAPTER I.

FROM HOME TO ST. LOUIS.

The 33d Iowa Infantry Regiment was organized under the Presidential call of June, 1862, for additional volunteers to aid in putting down the Great Rebellion. The number and place of rendezvous of the regiment were designated, with those of other regiments from the State under the same call, by proclamation of GOVERNOR KIRKWOOD; and after some uncertainty, SAMUEL A. RICE, of Oskaloosa, then Attorney General of the State, was appointed its colonel.

The mean date of the filling up and organization of the companies was about the 20th of August. The companies which, some time after reaching rendezvous, were lettered as A, I and G, were from Marion County; B, F and H from Keokuk County, and C, D, E and K from Mahaska County. The roll of the regiment in full, will be found in the Appendix.

The manner of organizing the companies was much like that used for other regiments. Persons more than ordinarily patriotic or ambitious, obtained recruiting commissions from the Governor, and by personal solicitation among their

2

acquaintances and others, obtained the requisite number of enlistments. Public meetings were held; and the already deep and intense patriotic excitement was fanned and strengthened by speeches, songs, martial music, and all other available and proper means. But a brief effort was required. In most cases, those who had recruited the companies received, by common consent, the first positions, and the remaining company-officers were filled by election.

The Fair Grounds just north-west of the city of Oskaloosa, were selected as the place of rendezvous, and named Camp Tuttle, in honor of Brigadier-General J. M. TUTTLE, of Iowa. Within the first week of September all the companies arrived there; and in a few days each of them had erected its own barracks, from lumber furnished by the Government. The barracks were of uniform style:—square, or nearly so; of rough boards, unpainted, without floors, windows or chimnies, and lined around the inside with tiers of bunks. Each barrack contained one company.

The first duty of the regiment was to learn the drill. With no previous military experience, Colonel Rice applied himself to the study of the regulations and tactics with such intense and unremitting attention that he soon made himself an excellent drill-master; and he always gave his personal care and effort to the instruction of the regiment. From four to eight hours a day were devoted to this; and it was not long till the result was apparent in the discipline and proficiency of the command.

Meanwhile, there were frequent parties of visitors to camp—the relatives and friends of the regiment; and the good cheer and delicacies that so abounded then were remembered many a time afterward, when the perils and privations of a soldier's life were no more prospective, but present realties. There was very naturally, much grumbling at the fare and circumstances in Camp Tuttle; but after the regiment had seen a year or two of active service, and knew what hardships really were, it was a common remark among us that if we were only back at Camp Tuttle, we would make ourselves comfortable as clams at high tide.

Late in the afternoon of the 4th day of October, our regiment was mustered into the United States service, by Lieutenant Chas. J. Ball, of the Regular Army. It was an impressive scene. The day was clear and beautiful; and as the mellow rays of the sun approached more nearly to the horizon, the men were drawn up in long double lines in camp, and the necessary examinations followed. Several who were now rejected, were nevertheless determined to go with us; and did go with us, and made as good and efficient soldiers as any of the rest. The examination over, the clear and ringing voice of Lieutenant Ball pronounced the oath of enlistment, the upraised hands fell to the position of "attention;" and the 33d Iowa Infantry, was part of the great United States Army.

As speedily as possible the regiment was supplied with clothing, arms and equipments. The guns first furnished were the smooth-bore muskets, which some months afterward were exchanged for Enfield rifles. A brass band, under the leadership of acting Drum-Major A. L. Ellis, was organized and put on drill; and it continued to play, upon occasion, until the commencement of the Yazoo Pass Expedition, when it failed entirely; and from that time all attempts to revive it, or to organize another, proved utterly unsuccessful—or rather, there was never much earnest effort made in that direction. Our dress-parades in Camp Tuttle were frequently attended by crowds of spectators; and often the line of the battalion itself would be so long there was not room for it inside the camp-ground. Greatly in contrast with this was the thinned and shortened line which remained to us after three years of service.

On Thursday morning, the 20th of November, we left Camp Tuttle, under orders "for active service in the field." A large concourse of relatives and friends had gathered to say good-bye. Such partings come but once in a life-time,

"Who could guess
If evermore should meet those mutual eyes?"

But cheerfully, buoyantly, the regiment marched away, strong in the consciousness of a great and noble cause. If they should return, this day would yet be re-called with pride and pleasure; if they should fall—but that they left to Him who guides the destinies of nations and of men.

The march to Eddyville, ten miles, over a muddy road, under knapsacks which bore down heavily on unaccustomed shoulders, was one of the hardest we ever had. Taking the cars at Eddyville we reached Keokuk that evening; and at about ten P. M., to the music of our brass band playing on the deck of the steamer *Northerner*, we bade adieu to Iowa. Now came our first experience of that stowing away of soldiers like freight in a boat, which afterward became so familiar that nothing better was expected. Yet that very stowing and packing away of human beings in this manner, even leaving entirely out of view the greatly increased risk of accident, has caused more suffering and death than many a hard-fought battle.

Passing down the river without any very remarkable incidents, we reached St. Louis in the night of the 21st. Colonel Rice reported to Major-General Curtis, then in command there; and next morning we marched through town up to Schofield Barracks, near Fremont's residence, on Chateau

Avenue. Accustomed to the manifestations of interest at Oskaloosa, we were somewhat vexed that there was almost no appearance of welcome for us in St. Louis. But General Curtis, as we marched past him in cadenced step of regular rythmic fall, complimented the appearance of the regiment very highly.

For want of room, Companies G and B were separated from the rest, and assigned to quarters two or three squares distant. Company H was detailed on provost-duty; and the remainder of the regiment was put on guard at the Gratiot Street and Myrtle Street Military Prisons, under the general supervision of Colonel Rice. The duty was rather hard for raw soldiers; and soon there was much sickness in the regiment. The condition of the barracks—which, heated up at night, grew cold and chilly before morning—was undoubtedly one of the causes of disease.

Drills came once in a while, and parade occasionally; but guard-mounting was by far the most important ceremony of the day. The pass system was somewhat strict; but most of us found means, nevertheless, to circulate about town quite freely. There were but few excesses committed, however; and the regiment was much praised, as the most quiet and orderly one that had been in the city. So passed our brief period of "fine soldiering." There was hard duty here, in some respects, but there was "style" and convenience; and the days of really "active service" were yet to come.

CHAPTER II.

FROM ST. LOUIS TO HELENA.

Saturday night, the 20th of December, we lay down in our bunks to sleep, as usual. Thoughts of the pleasant soldiering in the city, yet in store for us, were common in many minds, as it seemed to be the general opinion that we would remain in St. Louis, for some time. But about mid-night a "change came o'er the spirit of our dreams." There was a general waking-up in the barracks; and the cause of it was an orderly, going the rounds to notify the regiment to "be ready to leave, to-morrow morning at 8 o'clock, for down the river." Active service was coming now. Well, no regiment was more ready or able for it than we.

Next morning hurried letters were written home, ere we left what seemed to us our last hold on civilization; and at 8 A. M. we embarked on board the steamer *Rowena*. In the morning of the 24th, we landed at Columbus, Kentucky. An attack was expected here, and we were to help repel it. Piling overcoats and knapsacks on the levee, we marched out on the "bottom" below town, and formed line of battle. Remaining in line till about the middle of the afternoon, we were ordered to throw up breast-works. At this, our first attempt toward fortification, we worked faithfully till some time in the night, and then tumbled down to sleep, without shelter, as we were.

Things now began to seem, to us green hands, very much like soldiering. To make the case more agreeable, a heavy rain fell during the night; and next morning the ground we slept on was several inches under water. The hydrostatic bed may be a great luxury, but doubtless much depends on the manner in which the principle is applied.

Next day was Christmas. We passed it in waiting for the attack, but no attack came. Mr. Forest seemed to have changed his mind. In a few days our new wedge tents were erected, and we were therefore better fixed. But on New Year's morning, the regiment was ordered out to Union City Tennessee, to meet an attack expected there. After our arrival there, in the evening, the alarm was sounded, all rushed to arms, and battle seemed imminent, but nothing really happened. Some firing by our own men was the cause.

Union City was a nice little place, and our men remembered it with pleasure. Perhaps, one reason of their liking, was the fact that it abounded with meat, chickens, bread, potatoes and other eatables; and we there took our first lessons in foraging—lessons well learned and fully remembered, to the sorrow of many a sneaking old rebel who was "just as good a Union man as any body."

While there, one of our men accidently shot off the end of his finger; and Doctor Scott, our assistant surgeon, was called on to amputate it. Having none of the customary instruments at hand, the doctor immediately seized a chisel and mallet, and performed the operation at a single blow. Much fun was made of it afterward; but the actual results were apparently as satisfactory as though the amputation had been done in the regular professional way.

Companies A, F and I, were stationed out about a mile from Union City, to guard a bridge, until the 3d of January, 1863, when the whole regiment returned to Columbus. On the 7th we were ordered to leave, and struck tents and got ready. After waiting for some hours, contrary orders were received, the tents were put up again, and we staid till morning.

Then, being stowed away on the steamer *John D. Perry*, we started to follow the general progress of the war, down the river. About noon of Sunday, the 13th, we reached Helena, Arkansas, which place some of the boys profanely denominated "Hell-in-Arkansas"—a name more intimate acquaintance, inclined to justify; and leaving the boat as soon as we could, in mud and discomfort, we pitched our tents on a devastated garden in the center of the town.

Next morning a more suitable place having been found, our camp was moved to the bank of the river, some half-a-mile south of town. Ordered from Columbus to form part of the expedition then organized to move against Arkansas Post, our regiment had arrived at Helena behind time; and as the Post was then too nearly stripped of defense, Colonel Bussey, the commandant, detained us there.

Mud and misery were now the order of the day, with rain, snow, cold and discomfort for variations. We wondered if it always stormed at Helena. On the 24th, orders came for us to prepare five day's cooked rations, and hold ourselves in immediate readiness to start for Vicksburg. The next day, Sunday, saw us busily occupied all the time in cooking meat, baking up the flour already issued, and generally getting ready. The boats were there, the order was positive, and we were sure the wishes of many of us to "get into an actual battle and see how it seemed" were likely to be realized. But we never started, some thing or other changed the state of the case, and there we remained.

These were not the most pleasant days in the world, even for soldiers. Though it seemed to rain most of the time, yet the cold was frequently severe; and for want of any better accommodation, we had to go to the woods and gather brick-bats, pieces of wood, &c., and make chimneys to our tents. Teams were scarce—for us, at any rate—and we were compelled to go into the cypress swamps, some half-a-mile from camp, and bring up the wet wood on our backs, to burn. The mud was excessive; and as we were not yet provided with rubber blankets, and had not learned, by three years of soldiering, how to do without almost every thing, and "fix up" in any circumstances, we were of course decidedly uncomfortable.

But this state of things was not to last forever. While we were here, General Grant passed down the river to Vicksburg, with a portion of his army. The sight of the fleet loaded with troops, with colors flying, bands playing, and men shouting and cheering, was a new and grand one to us; and to the great displeasure of Colonel Rice, the regiment all broke camp and scattered up and down the levee, to get a better view. Full many a hour of extra duty was the penalty. Some thought this was paying too dearly for the first view of the "pomp and circumstance" of war, when we soon found ourselves on a fleet, and part of an army, and helping too, though distantly, in the reduction of Vicksburg.

CHAPTER III.

CLEARING OUT THE PASS.

By inspection of the map one will see that the Coldwater River of Mississippi, empties into the Tallahatchie, and this into the Yazoo River, which enters the Mississippi, a few miles above Vicksburg. Seven miles below Helena, on the eastern side of the river, there opens from the Mississippi to the Coldwater, a narrow channel, called the Yazoo Pass. Two miles inland it enters a beautiful sheet of water, which from its crescent shape, is named Moon Lake; and apparently passing through the lake, it continues to the river.

The Pass, though very deep, is but about 60 feet wide on an average. Formerly, it is said, very small craft occasionally were run on it, transporting cotton and plantation supplies; but later, the State of Mississippi had cut it off from the Mississippi River by a levee, to prevent its overflowing the low and level country through which it passes. General Grant, finding it necessary to use all means for the reduction of Vicksburg, had determined to attempt to open a communication to the Yazoo River, through this Pass; and for this purpose an expedition was organized.

On the 1st of February, 1863, a small detail from the different regiments at Helena, went down and cut the levee at the head of the Pass. The Mississippi was then very high; and the swift waters rushed through the narrow opening so fiercely as to flood the adjacent swamps. On the 9th of the month, our regiment went down to Moon Lake, on a "mosquito boat" and small transports, to join other troops in clearing out the Pass, that it might be more nearly fit for navigation. The rebels below us had felled trees across and into the channel, to obstruct the expedition as much as possible; and these had all to be taken out. Raftsmen and lumbermen were in demand, and Colonel Rice's previous experience on the river, came in excellent play. Lieutenant-Colonel Wilson, afterward major-general, was the engineer-in-chief, and performed his duties faithfully.

This was now peculiar soldiering. Heavy fatigue-details were made each day, or twice a day. The men had to get at the logs in the channel, cut them in two, or get them apart in some way, and then fasten ropes to them, by which to draw them out. Brigadier-General Washburne, in uniform distinguished from the others, only by the star on his shoulder, gave his general attention to the work, and would at times lay hold on the ropes, and pull with all the power of a two-hundred-pounder.

To counteract the effects of so much hardship and exposure, rations of whisky were occasionally issued. Those of the men who did not drink, gave up their ration to those who did, and thus some of the latter got "gloriously fuddled." This was before the day of rubber blankets with us; and we had to sleep on the ground, or on such flooring of weeds, cornstocks, boards, &c., as we could gather, with only our woolen blankets for shelter. Rain was abundant. But once in two weeks were there twenty-four consecutive hours of dry weather. Under foot was mud and water, and that continually.

Small boats accompanied us, bearing the rations, headquarters, &c. Of these boats, the *Hamilton Belle*, an old Keokuk ferry-boat, seemed most undaunted and serviceable. Her draught was so light, and her power so great, we used to say she could run in a furrow on a heavy dew.

As the work of clearing progressed, we marched further down the Pass, through the woods and swamps. A part of the regiment one night started to move further down, and darkness overtook them in the midst of a swamp. No place could be found, out of water, where a man could lie down; and they had to turn back in the night, tired, wet, and grumbling, and hunt a place to sleep. But even out of discomforts they made fun. Their camp was chosen close to the brink of the Pass. During the night, one of the longest and slimmest men among them, the flag-staff of the regiment in fact, got up, in the dark and before he was well awake walked off into the deep water of the channel. Fortunately a good wetting was all the consequence; and great was the merriment at Jack's unlucky attempt to sound the river.

But the most cheering event that happened was the arrival of the mail. None but those who have been in similar circumstances can imagine how anxiously each one waited to hear his name called when the letters were distributed, or how great was his disappointment at learning there was nothing for him. Words of love and fond remembrance may seem but little to their writers, but to him who is far away from all he loves, and surrounded only by discomfort and dangers, they are doubly dear.

Companies G and B were left behind the regiment for nearly a week, to clear out a particular drift. During this time a detail from these companies went out a short distance after forage, and several of company B were taken prisoners by a small body of rebels hovering near; but all or nearly all of them, were returned to the regiment before the expiration of our term of service.

This part of the country, swampy as most of it is, has some of the richest plantations in the State. We foraged a great deal. Beef was so abundant that sometimes cows were killed for the sake of the liver; for none of us were particularly desirious to be very saving of rebel property. The forwardness of the season seemed odd to us, when we thought of the time of the year. In one of our camps there was a peach tree in full bloom on the 14th of February. Letters we wrote in the midst of budding Spring would reach home a month later, in the snows of mid-Winter.

On the afternoon of the 18th, Companies G and B were ordered a few miles further down the Pass, to Alcorn's plantation, to re-join the regiment, as there was supposed to be some danger of a rebel attack. Reaching Pettit's plantation about dark, they made arrangements to camp for the night, and went to work to cook their suppers; but just as they were about to commence eating, a renewed and more urgent order came, and they had to start off supperless. That was a queer march, in utter darkness, in single file along the narrow top of the levee which was the most practicable road just then; but it ended at last, in General Alcorn's cotton-press, where the rest of the regiment was camped.

Next day we took formal possession of the general's negro-quarters, one company to a hut. Now came a general cleaning-up-time, our first for two weeks; and most of us experienced what is generally considered one of the last stages of poverty —washing our only shirt, and going to bed while it dries.

"Hard-tack" had now entirely lost its novelty, and almost any thing else was welcomed instead. An old negress on the plantation had a quantity of meal; and the regiment kept her overwhelmingly busy, baking corn bread, at 25 cents a pone. Frequently the door of her cabin would be crowded three deep by hungry soldiers waiting for their chances to buy.

The old general had a small corn-mill in his cotton-press, rigged to be worked by mule-power. At first, for some cause or other, the mules were not to be found; so the men laid their shoulders to the wheel by turns, and trotted merrily round the track, to grind their corn. It was a hard way of serving the country, however; and when at last the mules were found, they were put at work with little rest or mercy.

The Pass being now cleared out, there was other work before us. After some delay which seemed to us unnecessary, we went on board the *Hamilton Belle* and another small boat, on the morning of the 23d; and before night reach Helena, and entered our old camp there, glad enough to get back to it. But our rest was not long.

CHAPTER IV.

THE YAZOO PASS EXPEDITION.

On the 24th of February, we received two month's pay—the first installment since we were mustered in; and on the evening of the same day we embarked on the fleet that was to convey us down the Pass. Part of the regiment went on the steamer *Citizen*, and the remainder, with head-quarters, on the *Lebanon No.* 2. Brigadier-General Clinton B. Fisk, was in command of the brigade. The fleet consisted of two iron-clad gun-boats, a mortar-boat, and a number of small transports.

As the boats were to be our camp for some time, and we were going through the enemy's country, preparations were made accordingly. Each company was assigned to some definite portion of a boat. One would have the guard of one side of the cabin deck, from the wheel-house to the bow, another the corresponding place on the other side, a third the bow of the boiler deck, and so on, the room being calculated roughly to give the men place merely to lie down. On the hurricane-decks, breast-works of thick plank, were erected, and sharp-shooters daily stationed behind them.

Of course, there was little or no chance for cooking; there almost never is any, for soldiers on a transport. Coffee was made, "cold-pressed," as it was called, by turning on hot water from the engines; and when the boat stopped, or the engineer wanted to show his importance, even that could not be obtained. The meat-ration was cooked by thrusting frying pans full of it, in at the boiler-fires. About meal-times, dozens or more of men stood waiting their turns for this. Some cooked their pork by holding it on sticks over the escape-pipes of the boats. At times, however, the fleet would stop, when the men went ashore to do as much cooking as might be done at once. The officers in the cabin fared at the boat's table, of course; but the men were not permitted to buy their meals there. After a while the amazing ration of "hard-tack and sow-belly" became almost unendurable. From so long confinement to the boats, without exercise, the digestion became impaired. Men would sit by a box of hard tack and gnaw away at it all day, and lie down tired and hungry at night. Often some poor fellow might be seen looking in at the cabin door, at dinner-time, and wishing he had been born an officer, or even a cabin-negro on a steam-boat.

The country through which we passed was mostly swampy, and at that time overflowed with water; but there were frequent plantations, with negro-quarters, that looked like little villages. Rebel guerrillas were all around us, though not daring to show themselves much. On some of the boats men were wounded and killed by shots from the shore, but our regiment fortunately escaped injury from them.

The Pass and the Coldwater and Tallahatchie rivers are all very narrow, but deep, like most Southern streams. Our fleet was compelled to go very slowly, on account of the abrupt bends, swift current, and over-arching trees. The average speed made was about three miles an hour. Perhaps the best pilots in the world could not have saved the boats from injury;

but we thought the pilot of the *Citizen* was a rebel and wanted to smash the boat up. Often there were murmurs about the propriety of shooting him, when, at some sudden bend, or other danger, we would hear his old, familiar, careless cry—"Give her a turn back, Dan." The *Citizen* was a stern-wheeler, and somewhat unwieldy; and before the expedition returned, she had lost most of her "gingerbread-work," and was otherwise much injured. In fact, nearly or quite all the boats suffered more or less from the "rakes," as they were called, when they would swing into the current and hit the over-hanging limbs of the trees on the bank. There were many such "rakes" on the *Citizen*. One of them tore off a good part of the guard where Company B was stationed; and soon afterward another one come near "cleaning out" Company G, on the other side. Hats, knapsacks, guns and accouterments were left hanging in the tree as we passed. It seems almost miraculous that no injury was done to life or limb by these tremendous collisions; but the men soon learned to jump and dodge quite nimbly.

The Tallahatchie is perhaps the crookedest river in creation. It is so unearthly crooked that, standing on one boat of our fleet and looking at the others, one could not possibly tell whether they were ahead of him or behind him. In one place there was but just one foot width of ground between the Tallahatchie river on one side and the same river on the other, and yet it was perhaps a mile around the bend. Dense canebrakes occasionally lined the banks, and sometimes the boats would run into them a little, as if bent on crossing. There was occasional wet weather, of course; when those who slept on the hurricane decks had the disadvantage. They could shelter themselves very well, with their new rubber blankets, from the rain itself as it fell; but when enough water had collected on the decks it would run off in streams, and "wash them out." It is not the pleasantest thing in the world to be waked in the middle of a pitch-black night by a stream of cold water running down one's back, and thus to waken from the sweet dreams of home and comfort to find one's self out of doors and in the rain. But they would be young in the army who were not used to much worse things than that.

In the government of the fleet in emergency, a code of signals had been devised. One whistle, sounded from the head-quarters boat, meant "Form line and prepare for action;" two whistles, "Prepare to land and attack the enemy;" and so on. One night, on the way down the Tallahatchie, the fleet had run until it was too dark to go any further, and anchored in the stream, in the midst of an apparently endless and untraversable swamp. During the night there was a heavy storm of rain; and in the midst of it came the one whistle from the head-quarters boat; all was instantly in excitement, some doubted; but most if not all the companies were formed in such line as was practicable on the boats, and stood waiting for further orders. Of course, an attack was expected; and we wondered how it should come, and could not help wishing we had a more comfortable time for it. Soon came the other signal, "Prepare to land and attack the enemy." How to land, was the question. There had been no land in sight when we anchored, and now it was too utterly dark to see any land if there had been any to see. But orders must be obeyed, whether they can be or not. We were duly proceeding to do the best we could toward fulfilling them, when an orderly came on board, with the word that it was a false alarm. The whistle-rope on the head-quarters boat had got wet and shrunk, and so it "whistled itself." Perhaps that was the first time when a steam-whistle, without human agency, ever called a brigade of soldiers to action.

The negroes at the different plantations along the river greeted us with frequently the most extravagant expressions of wonder and joy. Doubtless they thought "Mass'r Linkum's boats" were wonderful affairs, and his men a wonderful army to bring them down there where nothing like the gun-boats had ever been before.

Great quantities of cotton had been hurriedly taken away before our advance, but we captured large amounts of it, notwithstanding. Before long, the rebels found themselves unable to get it away fast enough, and so they commenced burning it. One day our advance gun-boat came so close to a small steamer loaded with cotton-bales which the rebels were endeavoring to take away, that they fired it and left it to its fate. Cotton burns peculiarly, and for a long time. The bales were unfastened, and the burning cotton spread all over the surface of the river. Our part of the fleet passed along there at night; and the appearance was that of a river on fire. It was a strange, wild scene. Indeed, the whole Pass Expedition was a strange scene for us — in a strange country, where every thing seemed odd; and it was a very peculiar kind of soldiering any way.

In the afternoon of the 11th of March, our fleet reached Shell Mound, Miss., a few miles above the confluence of the Tallahatchie and Yulabusha rivers. The plantation had been recently deserted by its owner. It derived its name from a large mound composed entirely of shells, which formerly stood there, but which had been razed to the level, leaving small fragments of shell strewn over the ground. The mound was supposed to have been erected by some aboriginal race. One large mound, in the form of a frustum of a cone, still remained on the plantation, and its top shaded by fruit trees, was a pleasant resting-place.

Landing at Shell Mound, our regiment was immediately ordered out on what many of us supposed to be a march to battle, but which was probably intended for nothing more than a small reconnoissance, and was countermanded almost before it had begun.

Across the narrow strip of land separating the Tallahatchie and Yalabusha rivers, some two or three miles above their junction, the rebels had thrown a defense of earth-work and cotton-bales, which was called Fort Pemberton. This must yield before we could go further. Possibly the object, or one object, of our expedition may have been to draw the rebel force from Vicksburg. On the afternoon of the 11th, there was more exchange of shots between the gun-boats and the fort. Our regiment was ordered up the river a short distance, on the *Lebanon No.* 2, as a kind of foraging expedition, on which we twice fired a few shots at a small and rapidly retreating squad of rebels, and burned the plantation on which they were found. We returned to Shell Mound that evening. The fleet lying then in the bend of the river, with lights shining, bands playing and men scattered about, among the close and gloomy southern trees, made a grand, impressive scene.

Owing to the swampy nature of the ground, it was found impracticable to assault the Fort, and therefore there was not much actually accomplished. Regiments were kept out on picket, batteries planted, and other preparations made, but still there seemed to be no good opening for business; and on the morning of the 20th, our fleet started back up the river, on the retreat. That night a boat from Helena, brought us a mail, which came like an angel's visit to us wanderers in a strange land.

While we were on the way up the river, General Ross, who commanded the expedition, was superseded by General Quimby. Turning around immediately, we started back down stream, and reached Shell Mound again, on the 23d. In a day or two, a regular camp was formed—our brigade camping on less space, probably, than ever brigade camped on before. During the night of the 28th, a heavy wind blew down a very large tree, which fell on a tent in the camp of the 47th Indiana, and killed four men and wounded several others. After this there seemed to be among our officers a kind of horror of camping among trees.

General Quimby didn't take Fort Pemberton much more than General Ross did. We were occupied in standing picket, and planting batteries and changing them, until April 4th, when the whole force was ordered up the river again, on the final retreat. No remarkable event happened on the way. One or two plantations—or rather, the buildings and fences on them—were burned, in punishment of occasional shots from the shore near them. The fuel for the boats being now exhausted, landings were occasionally made, and all the rails in the neighborhood brought on board. A kind of rule was adopted in these cases, that whoever went ashore should not return to the boat without a rail; and the General would obey it cheerfully, bringing up the heaviest rail he could get, on his shoulders, though such a proceeding was very much beneath the dignity of some of the petty officers.

Occasionally the men amused themselves by nailing strips of boards, like guide-boards, to the trees, against which the boats were all the time rubbing. On some of them were hung bottles, old clothes, effigies, &c., at which our children may look, perhaps in after years, and wonder how they could have ever been put away up there among the limbs of those tall trees. When our boat reached the Mississippi river, we fired a "grand salute" of all the muskets on board, and the one six-pound brass field-piece on the bow—as a kind of greeting to the noble river. Cramped up as we had been for almost six weeks, on the narrow rivers in the swamps, it gave us a great feeling of relief, to come out again on the broad Mississippi, where there was room enough to breathe. On the afternoon of the 8th of April, we reached Helena; and next day pitched camp on the side of the hill afterward known as Battery A, about a mile north-west of town.

And so ended the expedition. In some respects it was the hardest of our soldiering. Even when men have plenty of the roughest exercise, the army ration as usually issued, is not very well calculated to continue health; and when men are confined so closely on boats, and almost totally deprived of exercise, as we necessarily were, ill consequences must be expected. Diarrhea was universal, almost unanimous. Few of us remained in as good health as usual, and many contracted diseases to whose sad end the lonely grave-yard on the bare Helena hills, within the next few months bore witness.

The whole expedition was peculiar. It was hazardous as can well be imagined. Had the water suddenly subsided while we were down in the swamps, as it soon afterward did, we should have been left at the mercy of a much inferior foe. There was danger all the time, and in many ways. The whole time seemed to us more dream-like and distant, when we re called it to mind, than any other period of our soldiering; and those of us who have been spared to read, in peace and quiet, here at home, these records of our army life and scenes, can hardly retrace, without peculiar feelings, their memories of the Yazoo Pass Expedition.

CHAPTER V.

AT HELENA.

In camp again now, in a dry and comparatively healthy situation, we made preparation for a considerable stay. The camp was arranged in as good order as possible, kept thoroughly "policed." Company A was detailed on provost-duty in town, from the 14th of April to the 25th of May. The regiment was put under a thorough course of drill again. Our field-music, which had almost entirely dwindled down to nothing, was started up now in such a way that it did not fail again until near the close of our service. There was a general revival of discipline and drill. On the 16th of April, the welcome countenance of the pay-master appeared, and we received four month's pay. The first time our brigade was ever out in line together, was on Thursday, P. M., the 30th, when Thanksgiving services were held in military order on our drill-ground. General Fisk, commanding the brigade, and Colonel (afterward General) Pyle, made some remarks and offered prayer, which were all our observance of the day.

On the 1st of May there was a slight skirmish between a party of 500 rebel cavalry, of Dobbins' Regiment, which was generally prowling around Helena, and a small portion of the 3d Iowa Cavalry, in which the latter was defeated. Our regiment was immediately ordered out after the rebels; marched out some eight or nine miles west of town; found no rebels, of course; camped over night in a rather pleasant place, and then marched back again. Drills continued, and the usual routine of camp. To aid the field-music in its marked improvement, a large bass drum was bought for the regiment, by contributions from the officers.

On the morning of May 6th, we started out, with two other regiments, a small squad of cavalry, and a section of the 3d Iowa Battery, for several days of reconnoitering. Colonel Rice had command of the force, and Lieutenant-Colonel Mackey of the regiment. Nothing remarkable happened on the outward march. Moving toward the south-west, we passed through some of the most beautiful prairie that ever was seen, dotted with pleasant groves, and covered with grass and flowers. Frequently our whole train could be seen at once, winding for three miles along the road; and the alternation of white-covered army-wagons and blue-coated soldiers, relieved against the dark-green back-ground of the grove or prairie, was pleasant even to wearied soldiers.

One day there was much fun and excitement over an unsuccessful attempt at capturing a very spirited old white horse which seemed to have the freedom of the prairies. Tired limbs suddenly gained new strength, to join in the chase; but even the officers' horses could make but distant approaches to the spry old nag. Great was the enthusiasm, nevertheless; and one could not but be reminded of Irving's spirited description of "Hunting the Wild Horse," on just such a beautiful prairie. At another time, while we were out on a large prairie covered with small sassafras bushes, there came a report that some rebel cavalry was close upon us. Our skirmishers were speedily sent out, our two pieces of artillery unlimbered, and we were immediately ready for action. But the supposed rebels proved to be only a squad of our own cavalry coming to join us from another road; and so we made much fun afterward, over the "Battle of Sassafras Prairie!"

On the 10th, reaching a large bayou, and without means of crossing, and having by this time accomplished the object of the reconnoissance, we started back to Helena. Tuesday, the 12th, was a hard day for us. Almost entirely out of rations, we had to march very fast, in order to get to town while we had any thing to live on. That night we had little or nothing to eat but parched corn. A rebel lieutenant, whom we had captured, made fun of some of us who seemed to think this hard fare, and said that he had lived solely on parched corn and slippery-elm bark, for months together.

On the 13th, as we started out for the march to town, the command was halted, and three cheers formally called for and loudly given over the first received news of the taking of Richmond! Alas! that it wasn't true. But like the story of the wolf, we heard it so much, before we were out of the service, that at last it found no credence at all.

At Helena again, the old routine returned. Our first brigade-drill was on the 18th; and battalion-drill, company-drill and skirmish-drill all the time, with the regular rations of guard- and fatigue-duty, left little room for idleness. There was an excellent drill-ground near camp, and we did not let the weeds grow on it. On the 22d there was a sham battle between the 3d Iowa Battery and the 5th Kansas Cavalry, which to us, who had never yet known a real one, was an exciting scene. Next day, Major-General Prentiss held a grand review of all the troops at Helena. There were on the field two or three brigades of infantry, three regiments of cavalry, and one or two batteries. This was the most orderly, sensible and satisfactory review in which we ever participated. Every thing seemed to go off according to programme.

About the 1st of June, there began to come rumors of an approaching attack by the rebels. Occasionally we would have to stand "at arms" from an early reveille till after sun-rise. One effect of all this was, that at last we grew to believe there would never be any attack on the place, and that all the long days of work on the fortifications, and the false alarms and every thing of the kind, were but the means adopted by our commanding officers, to keep us from rusting in rest. The fact was, however, the rebels had even then commenced moving from Little Rock, against us.

General Fisk having been ordered up the river, Colonel Rice now succeeded to the command of the brigade; and we never again had him for our regimental-commander. His life need not be written here. It is part of the history of our State. But we shall not cease to remember him as an able, zealous and careful colonel, brave among the bravest, of good and valued judgment, considerate of the welfare of those under his command, the model of an officer, and proud of his regiment, as it was proud of him.

On the 15th of June we moved camp to the bank of the river, a mile north of town. On the 17th, the old muskets we had so long carried were exchanged for Enfield rifles. The change was made in good time, as we soon discovered. The weather was now very hot, and the location supposed to be unhealthy; but we paid full care to cleanliness in camp, and as much to comfort as possible; and therefore got along at least as well as other regiments. And so the days passed, in the endless round of garrison-duty, with its "picket" and "fatigue," "picket" and "fatigue," in almost changless alternation, in the over-powering heat. It was by no means agreeable; but a change was near.

CHAPTER VI.

THE BATTLE OF HELENA.

The progress of the rebels from Little Rock to the attack of Helena seemed to have been well known to our commanders, or if not known, at least well guessed at; and our force at Helena was therefore kept well in readiness. There were frequent camp-rumors of the approaching attack, but few believed them. "Reveille at three o'clock to-morrow morning. Stand at arms till sunrise" became a quite frequent order; but these repeated appearances of alarm only made us believe less in the reality of any cause for them.

But the time came at last. At two o'clock, in the morning of Saturday, the 4th of July, we were called into line and marched down to the vicinity of Fort Curtis, the principal defense of the post, and there stood "at arms" for an hour or more. All was quiet; and though there was evidently "some thing up," many of us did not even then believe the rebels would seriously attack us; and some even doubted that there were any rebels there. In a short time they changed their minds.

Between three and four o'clock, in the misty light of earliest dawn, occasional firing was heard along the picket-line. In a few minutes it increased, and the alarm-gun from Fort Curtis gave the signal for the fight. Our regiment was immediately moved to the support of batteries C and D. The former was a little south-of-west of Fort Curtis, and the latter the most southern point of our western line. On the way to them we met Lieutenant Sharman, of Company G, riding on a horse, wounded, his face covered with blood. He had been in charge of the picket-detail from our regiment, which held the left of the line. A rebel brigade advanced against this feeble squad, and of course our boys fell back on the main line, but not until they had made such a gallant resistance that, a year afterward, at the battle of Jenkin's Ferry, some rebel prisoners asked what regiment we were, and upon being told, exclaimed, "O yes, we know you. You're the fellows that fought us so like —— at Helena."

During a momentary halt, while one or two companies were being detached for a particular station on the line, a sutler of some cavalry regiment, whose stand was near, brought out his stock of bread, cakes and pies, and scattered them among the men. And all day he kept his store open, with all he could supply of bread and water free to every soldier. This was not only a sign of sympathy, but was material and valuable aid; for we went out to the fight without our breakfast, a nd of course remained fasting most of the day. The greater part of the regiment got a share of the bread and water which were brought up near the line after the battle was over, but many had nothing to eat till night; and it is very uncomfortable fighting on an empty stomach.

The rebels attacked us with about 12,000 men, under Lieutenant-General Homes, Major-General Price and Brigadier-General Marmaduke, striking our ranks with their main force almost at the same instant along our whole line. But their most persevering efforts were directed at our left, which was held mainly by our regiment and the 33d Missouri. On the northern portion of the line, which was attacked by General Marmaduke, the 29th and 36th Iowa held the ground, assisted by a section of the 3d Iowa battery. The fight in this part of the field was not of so long continuance. On the southern portion the attack was repeated again and again, with a bravery amounting to desperation. All along the western side of Helena are abrupt hills, divided by numerous deep and narrow gorges, where in many places a man could only walk with difficulty. The trees that grew there had been cut down, and so disposed as to form the greatest possible obstruction; yet the rebels repeatedly charged over places where, after the battle, we could but slowly clamber in search of the wounded and dead.

For some cause or other, the whole left of the line seemed to be left somewhat to itself. Colonel Rice, in command of the brigade, gave his attention to the northern portion of the field; and upon Lieutenant-Colonel Mackey seemed to devolve the command not only of our regiment but of a good part of the line. Riding constantly from one end to the other, he distributed the companies as seemed most necessary; and so one company would be sometimes at one place, and sometimes at another.

Company C was stationed at battery C when the rebels made a grand charge and succeeded in capturing the battery. After a heavy loss, the company retreated a short distance; but the rebel triumph was of short duration. They attempted to turn our own guns against us, but a well-directed fire from Fort Curtis and battery D soon drove them back with heavy losses. The gunboat *Tyler*, steaming up and down the river and keeping up an incessant fire from her sixty-pounders, gave great assistance by the excellent "moral effect" if not by actual execution. The rebels believed there were several gunboats operating against them.

Under cover of the dense fog of the morning, the rebel sharp-shooters had crept up so near our ranks as to be very annoying to us; but when the fog lifted and the sun shone out bright and clear behind us, we soon made them seek a longer and safer range for practice. Our regimental-color was planted in the breast-work where the center companies were first stationed; and there it stood till the battle was over, when it was found riddled with twenty-seven bullet-holes.

In the heat of the battle some of us who were stationed near the colors, upon looking over to battery D, saw a hundred or so of our men go rushing out in a charge. Our hearts went with them as they gallantly advanced. In a little while they returned, bringing with them a crowd of prisoners of three or four times their own number. Oh! how we shouted then! Companies G and B of our regiment were in the charge. A brigade of rebels had advanced down into a deep hollow in front of battery D, and in coming out of it either way, exposed themselves to a raking fire. So our small detachment went and gobbled them.

A battle is generally supposed to be a time not only of carnage and death, but of grim and terrible excitement. But this was not the case in the battle of Helena, at least so far as our regiment was concerned. Our feelings were rather a lack of feeling. We acted and felt apparently just as though we had been in a hard battle every day of our lives. Up in the breast-works men would shoot at rebels as though aiming at buffaloes or deer. Laughing and chatting were abundant as ever. Officers would notice the missing shots of their men, and with all the eagerness of competition insist in trying a few shots themselves. Men would pick the best places for loading and firing behind the breast-works, and laugh at the close misses of the rebel sharp-shooters. Sometimes to get a better shot, they would raise themselves up at full length, thus exposing most of their person to the enemy. In this way private Jacob Miller, of Company G, received his mortal wound.

At the commencement of the battle, when the bullets first began its whiz scatteringly among us, we "bobbed" considerably. This "bobbing" is a purely involuntary motion, like the winking of the eye, when a foreign substance approaches it. Sometimes it seems almost impossible to keep from "bobbing," though every man may laugh at himself meanwhile, for doing it; but when the bullets come thick and fast the motion as involuntary ceases. There seems then to be no room to dodge. "Why don't you stand up straighter?" said one to a man who during a heavy fire of artillery, was crouchingly passing along behind a breast-work. "There isn't room," was the expressive answer. In the hottest of the fire, no one seems to think of dodging, but let the storm of bullets slacken much, and the "bobbing" immediately re-commences.

At one time during the battle there seemed some prospect that the rebels might at least effect an entrance to the town; but soon their advantage was lost in such way as to be worse for them, than to have never gained it. After repeated efforts, they slackened their fire, and finally drew back altogether. By 11 A. M., the battle was over; but our little force could not wisely do otherwise than remain in the defenses and await the renewed assault which all confidently expected. Thirty-five hundred of us would have looked scanty indeed, pursuing twelve thousand in an equal field. We did not know how badly we had beaten them. Had we but known the utter route and demoralization in which they withdrew from the field, we might have driven them to greater losses, or even captured the whole. But while we lay behind our works expecting, and ready for their return, they were rushing away in mad disorder, not even stopping to care for their wounded on the field. We had won a glorious victory; but it was obscured from public view by the still more glorious news from Vicksburg and the east, as moon-light is dimmed by the sun.

Placed in the front of the battle our brigade suffered the heaviest of the loss, and our regiment more than the rest of the brigade. We had 22 killed, 49 wounded, and 16 missing; and a large proportion of the wounded died of their wounds. The names of those who were wounded or fell will be properly designated in the roll of the regiment, herewith appended. Doubtless almost any other regiment, placed as we were, would have done as we did; but it was our fortune in this battle to bear the burden and heat of the day.

In the newspaper reports of the action, much credit was given to a colored regiment which held the left of the works, extending from the bluffs to the river; but the truth was that they were not attacked at all. If they had been, they would doubtless have done their duty bravely, but they deserve no especial credit as it was. The 33d Missouri was immediately with us much of the time; and from this grew a strong liking and cordiality between the two regiments. To pass through danger together is a great aid to mutual esteem. Indeed, it was noticed in the regiment, after the battle, that there was a much better state of feeling among us than before. Things seemed to move on better generally, and there was better discipline with less friction.

After the battle was over, we lay on our arms out in the trenches, to be ready for a repetition of the attack. Bread and water were hauled out from camp; but many of the men got none till well toward evening. The wounded were borne from the field to improvised hospitals, friend and foe alike, and received equal treatment side by side. It was remarked that the prisoners we took had very exaggerated ideas of both their own force and ours, many giving the former at forty thousand, and estimating ours at about half that amount.

One of the many personal incidents worthy of mention, is the adventure of Sergeant Moore, then a private of Company G. At one time during the battle, after an advance of a portion of our force, he suddenly found himself alone, and the rest of the party some distance behind him. Seeking the best route of retreat, he spied a rebel with a flag, and at the same time four other rebels with guns in their hands, who sprang to conceal themselves behind a log. Jumping to a stump, with that quick wit which in sudden danger, seizes the first available expedient for escape, he brought his rifle to bear upon a single rebel—who proved to be a surgeon—and summoned him to surrender himself and the four other men immediately. It was a bold demand, for one man to five; but Moore had the backing of a loaded rifle and full determination, and it didn't take the rebels long to see it. The surgeon surrended himself and the others, and Moore marched them back to the security of our lines, and delivered them up as his quota of the victory.

We lay in the trenches till noon of the 5th, but no attack came. A few rebel surgeons and nurses came in to attend their wounded. It was remarked that the rebels turned black almost immediately after death. Some supposed this to have been caused by the whisky-and-gunpowder mixture which was furnished them to drink, as remains of it were found in many of the canteens. Their dead were buried on the field; but since then the battle-field has been so changed by barracks and fortifications, many of the graves are indistinguishable.

We have spoken thus fully of this battle, because it was our first. There have been many vastly greater conflicts, but never greater victories. Thirty-five hundred men repulsed fifteen thousand, so severely they retreated in a panic, from the effects of which they never recovered. The "moral influence" here gained was of service to us afterward. Had there not been so much greater actions on the same day in other portions of the country, the victory at Helena would have rung through all the North. We would not wish the scene to be repeated; but now it has passed, there is no "celebration of the 4th" to which we look back with so much pride as our 4th of July at Helena.

CHAPTER VII.

THE LITTLE ROCK EXPEDITION.

The welcome the rebels received in the forenoon of the 4th, at Helena, was enough for them, and they did not think it advisable to return; but this we were not aware of at the time, and so an alarm came next day. We were lying in camp, trying to have a Sunday's rest after the battle, when the signal-gun from Fort Curtis, warned us again into line. Now we were mad. If the rebels had but waited a while, and given us some little chance to rest, we would have fought them again quite willingly; but we did not like to be so hurried about it. We made ready however, sulkily determined if the rebels came at us we would give them a worse whipping than before. This time our regiment was sent out just north of Battery A. Skirmishers were deployed, companies posted, and every preparation made for the coming attack; but no attack came, and no sign of any. Our commanders had doubtless happened to remember that "eternal vigilance is the price of liberty." Their caution cost us a very unpleasant night; for a heavy rain came on, and we had to lie in the mud, with only the shelter of our rubber-blankets. Returning to camp next morning, we again received the news of the surrender of Vicksburg, and again greeted it with three hearty cheers.

On the 8th a more formal and less unpleasant "celebration of the 4th," was ordered. All the troops at Helena, numbering perhaps, not far from five thousand, were drawn up *en masse*, at the east side of Fort Curtis, and addressed by Major-General Prentiss, and several minor officers, in terms of the highest congratulation upon their bravery and its glorious result. Just at the proper moment of the General's speech, when he alluded to the roar of the cannon on that day, which should be echoed again in more peaceful times in honor of the day, the guns of the fort and the neighboring batteries opened a fire that brought back the echoes of the recent battle. It may not be unworthy of mention, by the way, that this firing, as well as the cannonading on the 4th, was distinctly heard at Benton, in Saline county, one hundred and forty-five miles away—as we were afterward assured by testimony so concurrent we could not doubt it.

Again on the 10th there came another alarm. The signal-gun was fired, the long-roll beaten, the regiments hurried into line and marched to their appointed places in defense; the "pomp and circumstance" of war was marshalled in all its fullness—and in a little time three negroes were marched within the lines. "*Parturient montes et nascitur*" negro. The poor fellows had come from some where out in the country, hiding through the woods, and their sudden appearance at our picket-line was the cause of the alarm.

But finally, the battle and its alarms became an old story, and things settled down into about the usual routine of heavy garrison-duty. In a few days a detail from the different regiments was sent out on a scout; but they returned, with a report only of hard marching and some forage. Occasionally a boat-load of Vicksburg prisoners would pass up the river, looking very much like an animated clay-bank in the unvarying color of dirty-yellow. On account of the heat, the effluvium from the neighboring swamps, and perhaps other causes, our regiment was now reduced to an aggregate of only two hundred and eighty-five effective men. The pleasing presence of the pay-master enlivened us again on the 28th of July, and we were paid for two months. If there is any officer whom, *ex-officio*, soldiers are especially glad to see, it is the pay-master; and if his visits are not quite as welcome as those of angels, they are almost as far between.

About the first of August the rumors of a march across the country to Little Rock began to come in circulation, and frequently hinted at Texas also. In a few days they settled down into the plain facts that General Steele was to command an expedition against Little Rock, and we were to be a part of the expedition. Of course, there must first come a grand review, for which all the troops were formed on our old drill-ground, which was now so overgrown with weeds, that marching on it was extremely difficult. Previous to the march the sick were separated from the regiments; and this proceeding was to some a cause of great anxiety. Many manifested a cheerful willingness to stay. Some were excused by the doctors, who were fully able to go with the regiment, but to offset this, there were many who insisted on sharing the march, though pronounced unable to endure it.

At 2:40 P.M., of the 11th of August, our division, under command of Colonel Rice, took up its line of march. It was a hard beginning of a rather hard time. The heat was overpowering to us, who were unaccustomed to hard exercise in such a climate. Woolen blankets, knapsacks, extra clothing, &c., were soon scattered along the road. One big burly fellow in the regiment, after carrying his heavy knapsack as long as he could, began to haul it over and throw away a part of its contents; and among these he found an old ax-head, which some severe practical joker had slily placed there before we started. In a few days things grew worse; and on the 16th and 17th there was much suffering. The heat and the hard marching together, were too much for any ordinary powers of endurance. Men would fall out of the ranks and tumble down at the side of the road, by dozens and almost by hundreds. All such stragglers would have to come on after us, of course; but that is much easier than marching in ranks. In fact, marching with a regiment is one of the hardest ways in the world of getting along. A man may walk forty miles a day, alone and at his own gait and time, as easily as he can march twenty-five miles a day in the army. And a sick man, who can not march fast enough to keep up with the regiment, is frequently permitted to walk on ahead. This may be called a peripatetic paradox—that a soldier who can not march fast enough to keep up with his regiment, should rest himself by marching on ahead of it, yet such is often the case.

As we approached Clarendon, Arkansas, on the evening of the 14th, some of us, exhausted by the heat and hard marching, had fallen behind the whole column. Resting awhile at the outer picket-post of Davidson's cavalry, who then held the place, we started on again to overtake the regiment. Weak and weary as we were, every mile seemed almost endless, and every minute at least an hour. There are times when even a soldier may have some thing very much like "the blues." The more we marched, the less we seemed to gain; and darkness was fast gathering. Camp must be found that night, or our hard-tack and coffee would never do us any good. Still the town seemed no nearer. We began to think of "giving up" generally, and not trying to go any farther, when suddenly the rich tones of a good brass band greeted our ears. Had an angel suddenly stood in the way, we would not have been more surprised or cheered; and we pressed on with renewed vigor. It was dark when we reached the little huddle that bore the name of Clarendon. Davidson's cavalry were all over the place. Our division of infantry had just come in, "and passed on farther" some where, but no one could tell us where. One man would tell of their camping about a mile ahead, and the next would make them two miles distant; and after tramping over those weary miles the first man we met would tell us, carelessly, that the 33d was camped about two miles further on.

At last the camp was reached, but it was a labyrinth of cavalry and confusion. Of all possible places to "get lost" in, a cavalry-camp in the woods at night, is the most inexplicable. You lose your bearings, and there is nothing to show them again. You inquire, and the answer is more bewildering than the ignorance itself. You undertake to go straight across the road, and in three minutes you suddenly find yourself on the same side you started from. Your only resource is to get a darkey to hunt the way for you, or else to wait till day-light. We chose the former alternative; and the sagacious African piloted us through more twists and turnings than Cretan ever dreamed; and at last we reached camp, and soon forgot all present troubles in a cup of the soldier's true comforter, good, substantial coffee.

At Clarendon, General Rice appeared with the star on his shoulders, having received them since we left Helena. Sorry to lose him entirely as a regimental-commander, we were glad to see his sphere of service enlarged, and were proud of his success.

This Clarendon had never been a town, and had been burned some months ago, when General Curtis' army was there; so the little now left of the place was not particularly valuable nor attractive. Perhaps the spirit of the few inhabitants may fairly be judged from the fact, that one night during our stay, a secesh gentleman burned his own house to prevent its being used as a hospital for our sick soldiers.

At Clarendon we remained a week, waiting for orders, or rations, or "some thing to turn up"—we knew not what. There was much sickness, not only in our own regiment, but among all the troops. The march out from Helena, had been too hard for endurance; and beside this, Clarendon was the very home and head-quarters of ague in bulk and quantity. The very air was thick with it. We could almost hew out blocks of it, and splash them into the river. One morning one of the buglers undertook to blow the "sick-call"—a "quinine and whisky," as we usually named it; but before he had sounded a half-dozen notes a sudden ague seized him, and he was shaking vigorously. Another bugler took the horn, and he, too, had to lie down to shake. Lieutenant-Colonel Lofland came to the rescue, but the "sick-call" was too much for him; there was ague in the bugle, and he had to lay it down. At last came one more practiced in blowing, and by great effort he sounded the call; but while the rest went up to the surgeons' tent for their regular rations of quinine and whisky, he went off and spread himself upon the ground and took a shake of unprecedented vigor and duration.

By the way, there used to be a wonderful impartiality in the army some times, in the distribution of medicines. At any rate, the boys used to say it made no difference what a man's ailment might be—diarrhea, constipation, lameness, sore hand, gun-shot wound, or broken leg—the invariable remedy was the "C. C. pills;" and the boys would represent the doctor as occasionally ordering the patient, in his gruff way, to "take one every two hours, or two every one hour, I don't care a d—n which."

And there some how got into circulation the report, that when little Pete H——, stubbed and short as so tough a chap could be, went up to the doctor with some bronchial difficulty, the doctor opened Pete's mouth with no gentle hand, examined him with grim, professional carelessness, and at last gruffly told him that he had "piles or sore throat, d—d if he could tell which."

But to return to our ague: Comparatively speaking, the real, genuine "Clarendon shake" is to any ordinary chills and fever, about as a big bull-dog is to a pet poodle. We experienced it in all varieties and degrees; and the worst that any ague can ever do now for us, is to make us think of Clarendon. On Friday night, the 21st of August, the regiment started on, crossing White River on the pontoon. Then came a long stretch of corduroy-road, over which we had to march, in the almost utter darkness, first up, and then down, one foot off, and one on, stumbling and falling, and then scrambling up and tramping on again, till strength and patience were alike exhausted, and we believed that corduroy-road contained the oft-mentioned point "where forbearance ceases to be a virtue." If ever men were pardoned for profanity, surely those teamsters are partially forgiven, who drove their six-mule teams over that worse than road, in the darkness of that dismal night. And how mortal creatures, of limited capacities withal, can drive six indisputable mules hitched to an army-wagon, by a single rein, and wind around safely among stumps, trees and mud-holes, where a man walking must well consider his steps, is a mystery and a wonder.

Morning came at last, and a day of rest; and then we started on again. The country we passed over on the 23d, was so much like Iowa, as to be the theme of constant remark. There was Iowa prairie, and an Iowa breeze blowing over it; and the timber bordering it was like Iowa timber. Several times, in marching through Arkansas, we have found great similarity between the country there and some parts of Iowa, with which we were familiar. Indeed, perhaps, no greater similarity exists between any Northern and Southern States, than that between Iowa and Arkansas.

A little after sun-down, at the close of a hard march on which we had seen some suffering for want of water, we reached Duvall's Bluff, on White River, and went into camp. This was the 23d of August. Here was the terminus of the Little Rock and Duvall's Bluff rail-road, of which the rebels yet held the greater part, and which they had till within a few days been actively using. There had formerly been a few buildings here; but the expedition against Arkansas Post, the previous Spring, had destroyed them.

Here we remained a week in camp. The boats brought supplies up from Helena, and the mails came with tolerable speed. On the 31st of the month the onward march was resumed. Next morning we were informed that twenty miles of prairie lay before us, with no water except what we carried. All the way so far, there had been much difficulty in getting decent water to drink. It was the dry season. Frequently we had to go to the swamps, and skim a thick, green scum from the top of the water we were compelled to use for coffee. So we imagined we had already known what was meant by scarcity of water; but worse was yet to come. The well near us was exhausted, and no creek could be found. So scarce was water now, that to prepare for that twenty-miles march in the heat of a Southern August, many of us had to fill our canteens from a puddle where the hogs had wallowed, and in the bottom of which was a pile of bones.

That day's march was a hard one. The road was high prairie, and the sun shown down unclouded. Before the day was half gone, the "stragglers"—those who, from fatigue and exhaustion, were unable to march in ranks, and had to tumble down at the side of the road, and rest and wait—might be counted almost by hundreds. Many had drank too freely in the morning, and so too much reduced their scanty supply of water for the day. One hardly can imagine what thirst is until he has seen some such time as this, when he begins to have strange, waking dreams of water, and of the happiness of lying down, if only for a minute, on a green bank, and having a river run into his mouth.

It was well toward evening when we marched through the little town of Brownsville, and passed on into the woods near a bayou, to camp. The morrow was a day of rest, which the men improved in washing their clothes. Next morning, September 3d, at six o'clock, our regiment and two others were ordered out, in fighting trim, on a reconnoissance to Bayou Metoe. The weather was exceedingly hot, and the roads dry and dusty. This day's march was always considered in the regiment to be the hardest we ever had. The distance was twenty miles, and we accomplished it a little after noon. But many were compelled to fall out of ranks and wait till night before coming in to camp, or till the ambulance came and took them, if they were absolutely unable to travel.

Arrived at the bridge over the Bayou Metoe, the 33d was deployed as skirmishers. A battery of small howitzers, shelled the woods, but the only enemy was a small squad of rebels, apparently on picket. At night we withdrew, and camped on a beautiful spot, which had evidently been a rebel camp for some time. Ditches, bowers of leaves, portions of bunks, rude chairs, straw, remains of garments, old pieces of leather, stoves and broken boxes, were the tokens of recent occupation. The camp had been defended by a breast-work, from which General Davidson's cavalry had driven the rebels in a sharp little skirmish, a few days before. We found here two corpses of Federal soldiers lying in the woods unburied.

Next morning, by a march of less fatigue, we returned to Brownsville. The object of the movement out to the bayou had been to persuade the rebels that our advance was to be made by that place; and the feint proved fully successful. Sunday morning, September 6th, the regular march re-commenced. A part of the way was over a high and pleasant prairie; and as we marched we asked ourselves what the folks at home, at that hour attending church as usual, away up there in the peaceful North, would think if they were to see us wearily plodding along meanwhile, over those Arkansas prairies. In the evening, as it drew near dark, came one of those times when, as if purely from the innate depravity of things, the train seems to move but a foot at a time and then halt a minute. This is one of the most vexatious of experiences. It is more tiring and disagreeable than twice as much time at hard marching in mud and rain. And to add to the discomforts of the evening, the camping-place assigned our regiment was an old field, completely overgrown with briars, among which we had to pick our way and find room to sleep as best we could. It was a cheerless time; and perhaps the men were pardoned for part of the cursing. But at last the fires were kindled; and the fragrant coffee soothed each weary man to rest.

Next day the march was more agreeable. The road wound for some miles through the woods, where wild vines hung in greater luxuriance and profusion than we had ever seen. Grapes were quite plenty, from the small black frost grape to the rich and juicy muscadine. Emerging from the woods, we marched along the side of a field containing one thousand acres of corn, with a strip of sweet potatoes looking large enough to supply all our army while the season lasted. A New England farmer would scarcely be more surprised at the sight of some Western fields than we were at this, and some other Southern plantations. Here began traces of a contest in our advance, and they continued all the way. Occasionally firing was heard, as our cavalry drove back the rebel out-posts. The end of the journey was at hand.

CHAPTER VIII.

LITTLE ROCK.

The 10th of September was a day worthy of remembrance. The weather was clear and very warm. At about ten in the forenoon we moved out from camp. The train had been posted, guards detailed, and proper dispositions made for the expected contest. But our part of the victory proved very different from what we had anticipated. All day we merely marched along, making frequent halts. One place in the woods, where we stopped to rest a moment, seemed nearer the lower regions, by several notches on the thermometer, than any we had ever tried before. It almost melted the hair on our heads. Occasionally during the day, we could hear the rattle of musketry in the advance, which told us that Davidson's cavalry was still "driving them in." Toward evening the firing grew heavier and more continuous, and was varied by an occasional boom from the artillery. As we neared the ever-moving scene of action, it was with a constant expectation to be soon engaged ourselves; but it was not so to be. The cavalry did the fighting, and the solid columns of infantry steadily marching on, supplied only the requisite "moral support."

Reaching the Arkansas River, we could see how General Steele was flanking the enemy. The cavalry had partially crossed the river and advanced up the southern side. Wounded rebels along the bank were occasionally visible. Still we went marching on; and before sun-down we passed through the outer defenses of Little Rock, which the rebels had just evacuated in considerable hurry. The road was well obstructed, and the earth-works strong enough to command the passage. Here was where the rebels were prepared for us; and had not General Steele so surprised them by the Bayou Metoe feint, and the present flanking-movement, we should certainly have had some difficulty with them here. As it was, the pans and kettles, with victuals yet cooking on the fire, showed how unexpectedly they had discovered the position to be no longer tenable.

All the afternoon, smoke had been seen ascending from the direction of the city. As darkness came on, and we drew near the place, the fires were more distinct. The rebels were burning their cars and steam-boats, and some government buildings. An iron-clad gun-boat had ascended the river some months before, and the fall of the water had left it high and dry on the sand. It was now but a shapeless mass of burning ruins. The wooden pontoon-bridge, however, General Price had not time to destroy, though he made a hasty attempt to do so.

It was almost dark when we arrived opposite the city. The firing on the opposite shore had ceased, and there was a rumor that we were fully victorious. Still we kept marching on. The burning locomotives stood on the track a little to our left; and some one kept their bells ringing as we passed. Then, as the outlines of the city across the river became dimly discernible through the gloom, a horseman dashed past us, shouting that Little Rock was ours, and Davidson held possession. Loud rose the cheers, and that hour of our arrival opposite Little Rock, with its accompaniment of burning boats and locomotives, bells ringing, bands playing, and regiments cheering as we marched along, was one of the most stirring and poetic of our military life.

There seemed a kind of retaliatory justice in the time. The rebels had left this place, and traveled a month to give us a visit at Helena. We had traveled a month to return the call; but we were more successful than they. Some of our boys, taken prisoners at Helena, had been brought here for confinement; but before we arrived they had been paroled and sent to St. Louis, so we did not have the opportunity, as some had anticipated, of meeting and freeing them at Little Rock.

Camping that night where we first halted, our first business was, as usual, to make ourselves comfortable as might be; but next morning there was leisure for looking around, and wondering how long we should be there. Some sanguine souls flattered themselves with the prospect of a Winter in the city; but the more thoughtful rather expected but a brief rest in the great advance to Texas. So we lay and waited for the order which should let us across the river and into the city. There was much amusement over the story of a rebel surgeon, who had gone to sleep drunk, in the Anthony House, under Confederate rule, and waked to find himself protected by Federal authority, and who growled out his surprise that a man could not even take a little nap at a hotel, without falling out of the Confederacy.

On the morning of Tuesday, the 15th of September, we moved across the river and entered the city. The place assigned for the camp of our brigade was a gravelly and wooded ridge a little south of the arsenal grounds. Room having been allotted to the regiment, our first business was to make it habitable. The ground was covered with a dense under-brush, thickly interspersed with young pine trees. Though immediately contiguous to the capital of the State, it was as much wild land, as any in Arkansas; but it suited our circumstances very well. Our tents and extra clothing having been left at Helena, we now found it necessary to use all our ingenuity in making shelter for ourselves. The ground was cleared off, and large piles of brush were burned. One afternoon there were so many and so hot fires of burning brush that, though the day had previously been perfectly clear, before night a shower came on, evidently caused by the smoke and heat thus raised.

Brush-shelters were now constructed, and laid off by companies as a regular camp. Many of them were no inconsiderable protection. Of course they would not turn rain, but they were very good houses for warm, dry weather. Some of them were erected with much skill and patience. One man of the regiment, who "roomed by himself," kept at work for a week or two in twisting and weaving a kind of kennel in which to stay; and when it was done, and he was in it, the sight was almost equal to a small side-show at a circus.

Supplies were now to be hauled from Duvall's Bluff to Little Rock in wagons, as the railroad had no rolling stock in order. The consequence was, that we were put on quarter-rations; and very scanty living we found it. A great demand sprung up for pieces of tin and sheet-iron, of which to make graters whereon to grate corn. At these home-made graters the men would put in their spare time by turns, until they had meal enough to satisfy hunger for a day or two; and when that was gone the grater was in demand again. One or two small, portable, iron mills were erected, to be worked by two-man-power; and their creaking was heard at almost all hours, monotonous and dreary.

Near our camp was a garden, from which the boys occasionally "drew" sweet potatoes and some few other vegetables; but no body lived too high. Again and again we would run all over Little Rock in search of bread for sale, and find never a loaf. Pies of miserable quality and limited amount, retailed readily at twenty-five cents each; but eatables of any sum and substance, it was frequently impossible to buy. The city seemed quite deserted. Shops and stores were closed, and few citizens could be seen in the streets. Indeed, the ladies had been terrified by all sorts of wild reports about our army, until they dared not remain in sight of us. They got over this after a while, however. One who spent only the last week of our stay in Little Rock with us, could form but a faint idea of the appearance and manners of the city and its people when we entered.

The first part of our stay was by no means agreeable Scanty food, insufficient clothing, and such shelter only as brush-houses could give, were poor comfort, even after such a march. The nights were some times so cold we would have to get up before morning and warm ourselves by the fire. Teams were kept out through the country after forage, which helped out the provisions considerably; and some times those of the more fortunate among us could obtain meals at private houses in town; but altogether, there was not much in this beginning of our Little-Rock-life to make it's memory pleasant.

About the last of September, company- and battalion-drills were commenced again. On the 6th of October we received our tents and surplus clothing from Helena, and both were very welcome. The camp was now arranged in more military style, and to better advantage. The old brush-shelters were remorselessly abandoned and destroyed, and a general cleaning up ensued. In a few days, Mr. Scholte, of Marion County, Iowa, arrived, as commissioner to take the vote of the regiment. The election was held on the 13th, very quietly, at the Colonel's tent; and resulted in giving forty-six votes to General Tuttle for Governor, and all the rest to Colonel Stone. During the Fall, our boys who had been taken prisoners at Helena, having been paroled and exchanged, returned to the regiment. We were heartily glad to have them with us again, and the regiment seemed to them like home. Probably Little Rock seemed more agreeable to them now, than it did when they were there before.

Cold weather was now coming on, and preparations were made for Winter. Log-barracks were erected for the companies; and a great demand arose for brick-bats, sticks and mud, for chimneys. The town was ransacked for stoves, but with poor success. Only the Winter before, stoves had sold at one hundred and twenty to one hundred and fifty dollars; and people seemed to have hardly yet forgotten the old Confederate price-list. But soldiers "draw" things some times, and buy when they can't avoid it; and so before long, stoves and chimneys began to make the Winter-quarters quite comfortable. We now hoped to remain here quietly during the Winter—not that we had any desire to shirk duty; but it would have pleased us much better to have duty come in that way—and things seemed to indicate that such would be the case. But soon there came an unexpected, and not wholly delightful change.

CHAPTER IX.

WINTER.

At mid-night of the 25th of October, 1863, we were roused from our slumbers by the never-welcome sound of reveillie. Up and ready for action, was the order understood. Soon it was learned that the rebels had been making a disturbance in the vicinity of Pine Bluff, and we were ordered to Benton, a little town twenty-five miles south of Little Rock, to intersect their retreat. The hour of starting was fixed at two in the morning; and at forty minutes later we were on the move. Stopping about sun-down to take breakfast by the side of the road, we marched on fast and steadily till we reached Benton, at 4 P. M. A small squad of cavalry already held the place, and of course left little to be bought any where around there. But no sooner had we broken ranks, than there was a promiscuous scattering all over town, in search of bread and other eatables. The people must have thought the Union army was almost starved; and just at this particular time the opinion would not have been exceedingly out of the way. But our boys paid for all they obtained at Benton, and left the worthy citizens no cause for grumbling.

One of the "non-commishes" had been unusually successful in gathering provender, and had accumulated quite a pile of corn-cake at his place in camp. One afternoon he went out after more, and on returning he found two men posted as sentinels, walking a beat, arms at a "shoulder" with all due precision and gravity, before his pile of rations. Great was his wonderment, until he was informed that his personal grub had been mistaken for the regimental-comissariat, and this guard placed there in consequence.

On the morning of Thursday, the 29th, the troops started south-west—the 33d only, for a wonder, being left behind. We could only explain, by supposing it to be expected that the attack, if any was made, would be made there. But our detention was quite cheerfully obeyed; and the boys having all the town to themselves, had room to flourish considerably. The soldier never knows how long he may stay in any particular place; and experience soon teaches him, whenever he reaches camp any where, and sees no special probability of going further, to make calculations as if he were to stay a month. Many of our boys went around and engaged private boarding by the week. At one house where was a rather good looking young lady, who attempted to play on a somewhat time-worn piano, and sang rebel songs with such vim as only a female rebel can exhibit, there were some twenty or thirty blue-coated boarders—attracted perhaps equally by the cheapness and good quality of the victuals, the music of the piano, and the undisguised and spirited rebellion in the looks, words and actions of the black-eyed young lady.

While the fair weather lasted, it was all very nice to lie there in camp, and have no fatigue, and not much other duty, to perform; but on Friday night, while we were all sleeping quietly under our blankets on the ground, a heavy rain came on, and a hasty rising, building of fires, and general muttering and discomfort ensued. The next day, lumber was obtained in some way, and temporary sheds erected for the companies;

but of course, this was just too late to do any good. That night the other regiments returned from their scout toward Arkadelphia; and on Sunday, November 1st, we marched back to Little Rock. Very comfortable then seemed the log-shanties of our old camp, and very glad we were to be back in them. Now we could learn the truth or falsity of all the big reports we had been hearing; and they dwindled down to a reality of little, or nothing at all. Almost always, while we were out on the march, there would some how get into circulation, vague reports of the taking of Richmond, the defeat of Johnson's army, or some other great military event; and the truth would generally show no foundation for them.

Brigade-drills, and all the routine of camp-life, again commenced. Our brigade as now organized, was composed of the 29th and 33d Iowa, and the 9th and 28th Wisconsin Infantry. The command of it devolved upon so many different officers, during the period of its organization, it would be difficult to name the commander at each particular time. Occasionally, all the field-music of the brigade would unite for practice, and on some musters and reviews, played together thus consolidated. In this way, with from twenty-five to forty fifes and drums, squealing and rattling in unison, a "heap big music" could be made.

November 27th, we were paid off again, and the clothing account for the first year was settled. Some men had considerable money coming to them, while others, having just the same service all around, and apparently dressing no better, found themselves several dollars in debt. Our stay in Winter-quarters had now fairly commenced; and one day was so much like another, that no especial description is necessary. The main events of the day in camp, were guard-mounting and parade, which of course took place regularly, and with all the usual "style." Our part of the picket-line had always to be filled, and the customary camp-guard kept up. Details for fatigue were abundant. There was always some thing to be done. Either freight must be unloaded at the railroad depot, where all our supplies were now received, or there must be a forage-train sent out, or at least a detail to go after wood.

And so the days passed. The men in camp kept warm in the shanties, and amused themselves as best they could. Fiddles and cards were a constant resort. Some played chess, many read, and a few studied. The Library and Reading-Room of the Christian Commission, in town, though some what scantily supplied, were liberally patronized. Our ranks were now noticeably much thinner, than when we left home. Battle had taken some, but disease many. On the 15th of November, a recruiting-party, under Captain Lofland, then acting as lieutenant-colonel, was sent up to Iowa, where it remained till the next April, and obtained a number of recruits for the regiment.

By this time bakeries had been established in town, so that bread could generally, though not always, be obtained. The usual price for a loaf weighing a pound and three-quarters, was twenty-five cents. The army-ration is such intolerable fare for men in camp, that most of our regiment regularly bought a large share of their living, rather than sicken on the unwholesome "hard-tack and sow-belly." Potatoes could generally be had for two dollars per bushel, and butter at sixty cents a pound; and at such figures many a man spent the most of his wages in getting wholesome food. December 7th, Company H was moved out to a tannery, eight miles south of town, under orders as permanent-guard. They remained there until the 13th of March ensuing, having a very quiet time of it, and of course making some acquaintances among the inhabitants of the neighborhood.

The weather now in its general features, was much like that to which we had been accustomed in Iowa, but on a milder scale. A cold day was not so cold as in Iowa, and a warm day was warmer. The wind seldom blew so much at a time; and a clear evening was more beautifully clear. The moonlight was lovely, flooding camp and wood with a mellow, golden glory that made night more beautiful than day. There was no snow until the season was far advanced. The Winter was mild even for Arkansas. One morning—the 12th of December—we especially noticed as being exactly like one of our finest Spring mornings at home. Going down to the little brook that ran along the north side of camp, we could see fresh, green grass growing, and hear the birds singing in the trees as jubilantly as if Winter were forever gone. The pines looked bright and green; and the warm mist that rested lightly all around, had that languid, balmy, undefinable fragrance which we call "the breath of Spring."

Christmas came this year on the same day of the month as usual; and perhaps for this reason, as much as any, the boys observed it as well as they could. There was nothing public going on, but in camp there seemed an air of general jollification, and much provision of some thing extra to eat. A favorite dish was potatoes boiled and mashed, and heaped up in a plate, with a little butter at the top, "home fashioned;" and as the boys gathered around the rough tables, and saw the savory dish, many a thought went back to the homes we hoped to see before another Christmas should come. A dish of mashed potatoes is a very common matter; but like the Switzer's Ranz des Vaches it may touch a chord of tender memories. Some of the officers celebrated the day by a "treat" to their men. Company G was thus treated to an excellent dinner of roast pig and oysters; and other companies received similar attentions. Among the weary monotonies of life in camp, that Christmas of 1863 will be ever pleasantly remembered.

The 31st of December was such a day as might be chipped out of almost any Iowa Winter—a regular old blustering nor'-wester snow-storm, blowing all day. So the year went out, in cold and storms, and the new year came in, bright, clear and cold, like the eyes of a Northern maiden. There was no celebration of the day in our camp, for Christmas had exhausted the enthusiasm.

On the 8th of January, Charles Dodd was hung at Little Rock as a spy. Details were made from all the infantry, as guards to the execution. The criminal was a young man of scarcely twenty-one years, and had formerly resided only eight miles south of the city. For the last few months before the war, he had attended school at the St. John's College, immediately in front of which he now saw the last of earth. What his thoughts may have been, at this last terrible moment, no tongue can tell; but he bore himself with a bravery and composure that would have done honor to a better cause. This was the only military execution we ever attended. Many of the regiment would not go out to witness this; and the general expression of those who did go, was that they never wanted to see another man hung; yet the same men would walk unmoved, over the bloody horrors of a battle-field.

Company-drills were resumed on the 19th of January, as the weather was now mild and beautiful. Instead of cold and snow, and wind and storms of an Iowa Winter, we had warmth and sun-shine. But things were not all agreeable, by any means. For some cause or other, there came an unprecedented scarcity of rations. For several days about the last of January, not only our regiment, but most of the troops at Little Rock, had actually no rations on hand for several meals before the times of drawing. In our regiment a complaint was made to the lieutenant-colonel commanding, and an extra, or advance-ration was obtained and issued. The mere reading of the abstract statement that men were out of rations for a day or two, may not sound very bad; but the actual reality of going down to the mess-table at noon, and finding nothing to eat but a piece of rusty bacon, and having no means of getting any thing elsewhere, is decidedly a disagreeable matter to a soldier.

Some time in the Winter, a negro family of four persons moved into our camp: an old man, his wife, and two full-grown daughters. The old man built himself a shanty near the "sutler's shebang," and busied himself at whatever work he could find to do; and his wife and the two girls officiated as washer-women for the regiment. They were quiet, sensible, industrious folks; and in a little while a mutual friendship between the regiment and "Uncle Tony and Aunt Lucy," was firmly established. They would talk of us as though we were their brothers; and when the regiment left camp, or returned after a march, there were no truer or warmer words of welcome or parting, than those they gave us. Respecting us and themselves, yet knowing and understanding the differences of color and tastes, they attended unobstrusively to their own business, and were treated as civilly as white folks would have been in the same circumstances. If all negroes were like them, the social problem need never present a difficulty.

"Hard times," in a pecuniary point of view, are no less common in the army than elsewhere. There had now for some time been much stringency in the money market; but it ceased on the 10th of February, when the long-looked for pay-master arrived. General feelings of plethoric contentment pervaded the pockets of light-blue pantaloons; and the folks at home too, who had in many cases needed the customary remittance from absent husbands and fathers in the army, were gladdened by the money as soon thereafter as it could go. Perhaps few regiments equalled, and probably none excelled the 33d Iowa, in respect to the amount of money sent home. It was very common among us for men to thus send off so nearly all their wages, that long before the next pay-day they would have to borrow money to purchase needful food. Some managed to send home more than their wages; but they made the extra money generally by trading watches, or making and selling rings; a few made money by gambling.

On the 20th of March, several recruits arrived for the regiment. Fresh from citizens' life in Iowa, they came just in time to take part in some of the hardest, if not the very worst and hardest, of all our soldiering. It was a rough commencement of army-life for them; but in justice it must be said they bore it bravely, and seemed to get along as well as any of the rest. By this time, Spring with us had fairly come, and with it came a break in the monotony of "Winter-quarters." Active movements against the enemy were now the general order of the day, and we were to take part in them. The rest of Winter gave place to the activity and bustle of a Spring campaign.

CHAPTER X.

THE CAMDEN EXPEDITION.

The 23d of March, 1864, was clear and beautiful. Reveille was sounded at the usual hour; and at 9:40 A. M., with rations packed, knapsacks slung, forty rounds of ammunition in the cartridge-boxes, with all the paraphernalia of a long and dangerous march, to the old, accustomed tune of Yankee Doodle, we marched out of Little Rock — for the last time, we thought — as part of General Steele's column intended to join Banks' army at Shreveport, by way of Camden.

The march seemed harder at first, from our having been in camp so long; but we made the nine miles marked out for the first day without difficulty, and camped at night in an excellent place, on the Benton road. "A good camping-place" means a place where there is plenty of good water convenient for all the men and animals, plenty of rails, or other handy timber for fires, and enough of tolerably smooth ground to sleep on. How we used to hope for all these! and how often to the labors of the day were added much more at night, which might all have been avoided if we could have had a good camping-place! When no water could be obtained within half-a-mile, and no good wood was to be found at all, and the thick brush had to be grubbed away from ground enough to sleep on — all of which some times occurred — there seemed little show for comfort or rest at night. Add to this, mud knee-deep and a steady rain falling, and there is a picture of what soldiers call decidedly uncomfortable.

Next morning our bugle startled the surrounding darkness, and soon the call was answered from all the neighboring fields. Bugles rang as we had never heard them before. If an enemy had been in hearing distance, he must have thought we were at least a hundred thousand men, to raise such a wide-spread din. Finally a brass band, that accompanied the expedition, rang out its mellow tones, and the noise of the bugles ceased. The Camden Expedition started out "in style."

On the evening of the second day, camping early in a good place, we drew our first rations for the trip, and learned that during the march, but half-rations would be issued, except that with commendable care and prudence the General had ordered a full allowance of coffee for all the time. For this we always thanked him. Coffee is the soldier's friend. On a cold, wet night, after a hard-day's march, nothing is so eagerly anticipated, and so gratefully welcomed, as the soothing, yet stimulating coffee. Yet the army style of making it would make a woman smile with scorn. If a large amount is to be made, as enough for a company, a doubly-generous quantity of ground coffee is put into an iron camp-kettle, and left to boil till the strength is all out of it; and when this plan is not adopted, each man makes it for himself, on the same principle, but in a little tin can. The liquid in either case looks very much like the water of the Rio Grande, or of the Missouri "on a bender," but its taste is good, and its effects plainly perceptible. It is a thing almost indispensable in the army. Necessary as tobacco is generally held to be, and universal as is the use of it, if it were left to the vote of a division of soldiers, whether on the march they should give up their coffee to save their tobacco, the answer would be, after much and painful deliberation, "Let's take the coffee."

Perhaps those who never were in the service, looking at the "regulations" may find that the standard army-ration embraces quite a variety of tolerable food; and they may infer from that that living on half-rations is not so very bad after all. The "army regulations" are all very nice, and the army-ration would do very well for soldiers if they could only get it. But the exact amount of food that was issued to us as half-rations on this expedition was two hard-tacks, a little salt pork, a little salt, and some coffee, to each man per day. And this was not in prison or in camp, but on the march; and on the strength of this men had to tramp through rain or shine, good or bad going, level road or hills, with gun and rig, weighing from twenty to twenty-five pounds, and knapsack, haversack and other articles, weighing almost as much more; and this was a fair sample of our fare for months together. Is it any wonder men foraged?

Southern nights and mornings are always cool. The day may be oppressively hot, and the night so cold that the one woolen blanket which the soldier has hardly persuaded himself to carry so far, will not keep him warm enough to sleep. Frequently we had to "tumble up" from our beds on the ground at three or four o'clock, in those cold Spring mornings, and take the remainder of our rest in standing at the fire.

The fifth day of the trip, March 28th, our regiment was taken as train-guard — that is, divided up into squads of a company or less, and stationed along among the wagons. The day for this duty on the march was always counted as a tiresome and disagreeable one with us, for it necessitated slow marching, with an occasional hurry, frequent little stops, much fretting and impatience; some times a good deal of work in getting wagons out of the mud, and always a late coming into camp at night. This day it was about five in the afternoon when we turned off into the brush, as usual, to bivouac for the night. One who has never tried it can not imagine how welcome the camp some times seems to the tired and weary soldier. Of all fatigue, perhaps that of long marching is the most wearisome. It comes on by such slow, monotonous degrees, and there is so little change or relief about it, that one feels much more worn out after a hard-day's march, than after equal labor in any other way. So this evening, when we were filed off into the brush for the evident purpose of camping, and then had to march and counter-march among the stumps and brush-patches several times before our lines were satisfactorily adjusted, it may be supposed we were not in the very best of humor; and possibly there may have been some very uncomplimentary remarks made concerning the worthy major who commanded us during the march to Camden. But right upon this, adding worse to bad, came the order for our regiment to advance some three miles farther, to hold a bayou, at which there was supposed to be some danger of attack from the rebels. Murmuring rose, not openly but earnest, but of course we had to go; and the rest that night was none the less sweet, when we did get it.

The next day gave us some consolation, in laughing at the sorrows of others. A dirty, ragged old Dutch woman, whose house we were passing, came out obstreperous to us, and with loud words and lamentations, demanded to be directed to the "coornul." Being shown who he was, she besought him sorely that he would help her. Some Dutch cavalry-man in front of the train, had seen a horse in a pasture thereabouts, that was better than his, and had quietly made a trade by changing the saddle and equipments from his own horse to the other, and riding off, leaving the tired cavalry-horse, well pleased with the change. Such little swaps were common in the army, and recognized occasionally by the code of military necessity; but the old woman could not view the matter with our unprejudiced eyes. She wanted Major Gibson to signify authoritatively to the cavalry-man, that she rued the bargain. From a civil stand-point, her position was undoubtedly the correct one, but the major declined to take any definite action in the case; and so the old frau's uncouth rage and lamentation were laughed at by the whole regiment, as we passed. Doubtless she has to this day a very poor opinion of the Yankees.

About three miles from Arkadelphia, we suddenly came to a place, where all the trees, and the brush and grass looked much fresher and greener than any where else. The change was as great and noticeable as though the season had been moved a month forward, while we marched a mile. It had almost the appearance of magic. We never saw a similar appearance elsewhere, and could never account for this. The place itself was like a hundred others we had passed—a low, flat portion of the bottom-lands bordering a bayou, and surrounded by timber. Under ordinary circumstances it would have been pleasant, but then it was delightful.

In the afternoon of March 29th, the sixth day out, we entered camp in the outskirts of the fine village of Arkadelphia—a place which seemed to us much like a Northern town. Situated on the Washita River, and built mostly of good, white frame houses, it presented a very different appearance from many of the dilapidated "huddles" to which we had been more accustomed. Very soon after breaking ranks, our men were pretty well distributed around town, seeing the sights and searching for eatables. There was little, if any foraging done. We paid for nearly all we got; and the women of the place frequently told us, "Yur men treat us better than our own men do." A considerable amount of good ham, corn-meal and molasses was obtained. The town indeed seemed much better provisioned than we had expected, though there was no surplus of food. Many of the citizens were dubious about taking our money, lest after our army had left the place, the rebels should trouble them for having received it.

The regiment was pretty well scattered around town, and not all the men had got their suppers, when at a little before sun-set a most unexpected order came for us to pack up forthwith and march back to the bayou, three miles from town, to camp there as guard for the train, which could not all get across before morning. The order received at regimental head-quarters may or may not have stated this reason for the movement, but the order sent around to the companies said nothing about it. The men could not know the object of the march, or of what length it was to be; all they could learn was, that they were to pack up and move again. Wrath and curses rose loud and thick, but did no good. When we were once started, these ill feelings found better vent in whoops and yells that made the echoes ring. There may have been some need of hurrying, but it was more from a kind of vexation and half-conquered wrath that we struck into a march as fast as we could go, and kept on going faster and faster. The Major's old horse, at the head of the battalion, had to trot all the time to keep out of our way. The first two or three companies marched those three miles in just thirty-five minutes, and turned into camp at a pleasant place near the bayou; but the rear of the regiment was strung out half-way to town.

6

It is much harder to march in the rear, than in the front of a regiment or column; and of course, when the front marches as fast as it can, the rear must lag behind. But if any regiment can make better time than three miles in thirty-five minutes, in heavy-marching order, we do not know where it is to be found. The next morning it took us just one hour, of good, steady marching, to go back to town. Entering the former camp again, we looked for a rest of two or three days.

There was in Arkadelphia, a pretty good two-story white frame building, used as a seminary for young ladies, and furnished with desks, charts, maps, &c., and a very passable piano. Led on by the very demon of mischief, some of our men, with a number of men from other regiments, ransacked the building from end to end, tore up the maps and papers, destroyed the benches, and smashed the piano into utter ruin. The whole seminary was left a perfect wreck. The guilty parties were not discovered, and so our whole regiment had to bear a share of the odium of this most dastardly and abominable act of wanton destruction; and never before or since, was it concerned in such an abuse of military power.

The rebel General Fagan was reported to be hovering in the vicinity, with a force of about five thousand men. He would never have dared to attack us there and then, of course, but still we had to be ready for him; so our little army went through the farce of standing "at arms," one morning, for a short time.

At 8 A. M., of the 1st of April, we started on again; and at night, after a march of about a dozen miles, the camp was pitched in the woods near a couple of houses, which collectively, were designated in the geography, (if at all) by the romantic name of Hollywood, Arkansas, but by the inhabitants were ordinarily called Spoonville. Next day our regiment was scattered as guard among the train, and part of it was pretty well toward the rear. This was a hard day all round. During a good part of the time, there was skirmishing with a body of rebels, whose number we had no means of knowing. The field-pieces which accompanied the rear-guard were pretty actively employed with occasional shots "on the wing." Our regiment was not in any of the skirmishing; but two or three of the companies were kept double-quicking a good deal of the time, first to the rear as re-inforcements, and then back to their place in the train again. A part of the afternoon there were great efforts made to "close up the train," which had become badly scattered along the road; and the haste, and bustle, and confusion and fatigue so occasioned, were so nearly like what a stampede or a panic must be, that we hoped never to see any closer imitation.

Nearly all the way was through timber, mostly pine. Some of the time our advance-guard would set the leaves on fire before us, which compelled us at times to march for hours together, through the dense smoke and heated air of the still burning under-brush. This was dangerous business for powder-wagons and caissons, but fortunately there was no explosion. On the 4th of April, as we lay in camp near the Little Missouri River, most of the time under orders to be ready to move at a moment's notice, there was quite a skirmish down on the river, in our plain hearing, for about an hour in the forenoon. General Rice was slightly wounded on the head, several men were killed, and a number of prisoners taken, before the rebels were driven back from the river.

Resuming the march on Wednesday morning, April 6th, we crossed the Little Missouri, on a kind of impromptu bridge, and soon heard the first of that skirmishing in our front, which continued at intervals, more or less all day. The rebels were disputing our advance. At one time nearly our whole force of infantry and artillery was drawn up in battle array on an open place in the woods; and part of the day we marched in line of battle, with skirmishers deployed. There were frequent appearances of an impending battle, but the rebels steadily retreated before our cavalry; and after driving them a few miles, we turned back to a nice place in the woods, near the river, and went into camp. Here we lay until the morning of the 10th. A forage-train was sent out; and as it did not return at the appointed time, there was considerable anxiety lest it had been "gobbled" by the rebels. The seventy-five teams and four hundred men would have been a very good haul for Mr. Price; but he failed to get them that time. They came in all right, after a while, having met with no difficulty.

While we lay here, the long-looked-for and much-talked-of, re-inforcement of "Thayer's command" arrived, from Fort Smith. A nondescript style of re-inforcement it was too, numbering almost every kind of soldiers, including Indians, and accompanied by multitudinous vehicles, of all descriptions, which had been picked up along the road. General Steele toned down this extra-transportation a good deal before we started again.

On the morning of the 10th, the train commenced moving, but it was one o'clock in the afternoon before it was stretched out enough to allow of our taking the place assigned us. Before long the rebels began to resist our advance. All the way was through timber, mostly pine, and a good part of the time we marched through this, in line of battle. As we neared the large and beautiful prairie called Prairie De Anne, the opposition of the rebels increased. Their main body was posted on the prairie, under command of Price himself, and numbered several thousand. Our own force now, as we supposed, must have comprised between ten and twelve thousand men.

At about 4:45 P. M., as we came upon the edge of the prairie, the continuous skirmishing merged into a battle, and the artillery-firing became quite heavy. Our regiment advanced in column by division. At one time we marched in this close formation for several minutes, in the direct range of a rebel battery, whose shot and shell came nearer than we deemed imperatively necessary. A piece of shell struck Private Wm. P. Funk, of Company I, wounding him on the head so that he died in a few hours. There was no other casualty in our regiment during the battle. Marching steadily forward to the edge of the prairie, we were ordered to support the 9th Wisconsin Battery, which was done, as ordered, by lying down flat on our faces, in line of battle, while the battery continued its vigorous and well-directed fire. The rebels responded actively; but their guns were of an old and inferior pattern, and their shot and shell, though very destructive to the trees in the rear, did not come very near us. For a while the cannonade was brisk and lively; but it gradually grew weaker, as the rebels retreated, and before sun-down, had almost ceased.

Now began a slow and cautious advance over the prairie, in line of battle, with skirmishers deployed, and interrupted by frequent orders to halt and lie down. The prairie was at intervals intersected by small brooks, fringed with dense and some times very thorny thickets; but we advanced now, in scarcely broken line, through places where, in peaceful times, we would not think of forcing passage. As it grew too dark to go any farther, the line was ordered back a little, to one of these thickets, where we stacked arms for camp. The night was clear and cold, and our wagons had been left a mile or two behind us, which two facts caused the hearts of the officers to sink considerably, for their blankets, mess-chests, &c., were with the train. The men had all their possessions with them, of course, and could therefore eat hard-tack and drink coffee, and tumble down to sleep about as usual; but the officers had to get along as best they could. Many of them were compelled to stay awake and shiver all night, and that without their accustomed supper. It should not be understood that the men refused to share with the officers, but there was not enough of either food or clothing for all.

During the night the rebels kept up an occasional artillery-fire, aimed at us, but doing its only damage among the trees far in the rear. Those of us who were out on picket, could see not only the flash of their guns, and the light of the shells as they rose in the air, but the very blaze of the old-fashioned matches they used, instead of the improved locks or primers of more modern construction. So near were our picket-lines to those of the rebels, that much ill-humored conversation passed between them, the "Jonnies" being particularly severe on us for being all Dutchmen.

Some time before mid-night, we were suddenly waked by the fierce firing of small arms near us. The rebels were making a bold sortie, to capture one of our guns; but they were repulsed before we could even move toward them. Our sleep that night was too much interrupted to prove refreshing. Next morning, details of men were sent back to the wagons, to make coffee at fires kindled behind some thickets, which hid them from rebel view. The more fastidious also had their pork fried, and some went so far as to stew up crackers in grease and water, as a luxury; but the majority of the line had to take the "hard-tack and sow-belly" in a raw state, and be thankful to have their coffee warm. The remainder of the forenoon, we merely laid there, waiting orders. It was a beautiful day; and the singing of the birds in the thicket near us, contrasted oddly with the occasional booming of the cannon and the continued skirmishing on some part of the line. As for us, we hunted rabbits, played euchre, read old novels, wrote away at letters, slept, and so on, as though there were no thoughts of battle in the world.

At 2:25 in the afternoon, a forward movement commenced. The whole of our little army was drawn up in battle array, in such a disposition that it looked even to ourselves like a large force, and to the rebels in our front, must have seemed an utterly overwhelming array of infantry, cavalry and artillery. We heard afterward, that when General Price saw us thus advancing, he threw up his hands and exclaimed "My God! they are coming in clouds," and immediately ordered a retreat. Certainly it was to us, and must have been more to them, a magnificent spectacle. The vast prairie, with its beautiful diversity of groves and undulations, was just the ground for such a display; and we can not easily forget the enthusiasm awakened by the martial scene.

"To warrior bound for battle strife,
Or bard of martial lay,
'Twere worth ten years of peaceful life—
One glance at their array."

Toward evening we halted for some time, on the high prairie. There was considerable skirmishing in front. Captain Comstock, in command of our skirmish-line, advanced so near the rebels, that he was confident he could have captured one of their guns, if he had been allowed to go farther. Their old smooth-bore field-pieces threw shot so awkwardly, that some would plunge into the ground far in front of us, and others would come so closely down in our rear, that we began to have some fears of being shot in the back, though fairly fronting the enemy. Meanwhile, as if for relief from the monotony of lying still to be shot at, an old cow, with a bell on, started up near us, and was immediately pursued by some thing less than a hundred shouting and laughing soldiers, but finally succeeded in making a fair escape. It was but a very little matter to write about, yet it made more fun than ten times as great an event could have caused at another time.

That night we marched back to our previous camp; and before six next morning, our whole force was again in battle array, and advancing toward the enemy. The skirmishing was at times, quite lively. Our batteries would open on the rebels, and speedily silence and scatter them. At about 9 o'clock, we reached the edge of the woods, and entered the rebel camp, which their rear-guard had just evacuated. Over a mile of very passable breast-works, alternated with places for cannon, of such a range that they could have literally mowed us down in a direct assault, were now, with a choice of routes from there, in our possession, with hardly any loss; and we were much pleased at this result of a flanking movement.

Halting here but a little while, the column moved off across the prairie, to the Camden road, and soon after reaching that, passed through a town called Moscow, consisting of three houses, one of which had been in use as a temporary rebel hospital, and then contained a member of the 1st Iowa Cavalry, who had been severely wounded, and taken prisoner, a few days before. The orders against foraging were now very strict, and some of the officers—not of our own regiment—were very strict in enforcing them; but men on half-rations, scant half at that, will have some thing more than that amount of food to eat, if they can get it. Sugar, pork, chickens, pigs, &c., fell a frequent prey. Not always to the victor came the spoils. On one occasion, a boy of our regiment had shot a fine pig, by the side of the road, and was just skinning it, when the officer of the day rode up, and made him go off and leave it. During the confab, while the officer's back was turned, another of our boys, quietly walked off with the pig. So the only harm done, was that one mess had an extra camp-kettle full of unauthorized pig.

At one place in the woods, where a short halt was ordered, there was heard a low, continuous sound, like distant thunder, or a mighty water-fall. Attention was at once arrested, but no cause for the sound was visible. The matter bade fair to remain a mystery, when suddenly some one discovered that a large and hollow oak tree, a little distance from the road, had been fired at the bottom, and the sound was produced by the current of heated air passing through it, and escaping by a large knot-hole at the top. It was in fact, a natural chimney, with the best draft in the world.

At frequent intervals on Wednesday, the 13th, we could hear cannonading in the rear, where Thayer's Division marched. In camp that night, there were all sorts of reports concerning the losses of the day. Slightly exaggerated statements represented that one of the colored regiments had lost eleven hundred men and two colonels; but not many believed so much. Finally, all the reports settled down into the fact, that the rebels had followed us, and tried to annoy us all they could. Next day, the route lay through some of the worst swamp that ever was traversed by mortal man. Marching was out of the question, and wading through the mud and water, was the rule instead. The portly figure of the Major, rode at the head of the column, on an old raw-boned white horse, that waded with a mechanical regularity of splashing, until one unlucky moment, in the very worst place in the whole series of swamps, the poor beast stumbled and fell, and the Major went sliding over his head, with all due and perpendicular gravity, plump into the mud and mire. The performance had a tendency to damage fine clothes, but it did the regiment more good than a little; for it roused a freshness and jolliness of feeling that lasted till we struck dry land again.

On the afternoon of the 14th, General Rice was ordered to proceed with our brigade, with all speed, leaving knapsacks behind, to a cross-road, between us and Camden, which the rebels were endeavoring to reach before us. It was a forced march, and we traveled as fast as possible, actually drawing and distributing rations while on the move. We had expected to march all night, or nearly so; but as darkness came on, an unusual fatigue began to overpower us, and word was circulated that we would camp before long. Every mile grew longer than the rest, and still the march went on, with no sign of stopping. We were worn out, hungry, and longing for the brief repose of camp; but our regiment was some where toward the rear, and would not come in till most of the others had got there. "How far is it to camp?" was the question in every one's mind, but no one could answer; and so we jogged wearily on, in silence. At last a cavalry-man came galloping toward the rear, and as he neared us, he shouted "Three miles to camp! three miles to camp!" Seldom were words more welcome. We marched on with renewed vigor, and soon found rest for the night; but the shout of the cavalry-man made so strong an impression on the mind of one of our regiment, that he penned some lines in remembrance of it, which I may be pardoned for introducing here.

"THREE MILES TO CAMP!"

APRIL 14TH, 1864.

Onward marching, ever onward, through the forest, lone and drear,
Now fatigue almost o'ercomes us, scarce our limbs their burden bear.
Still the evening shadows deepen, yet no sign of rest appears,
But a horseman comes to meet us, and his glad shout greets our ears:
"Three miles to camp! three miles to camp!"
Pass the word along the column,
Cheer the weary, cheer the solemn;
Soon will rest come now, it's only "three miles to camp!"

Now with strength renewed, our footsteps measure off the weary way,
Till before us "rest and supper," bright the shining camp-fires say.
Stretched at ease, we then remember how the day dragged slowly by,
And how sudden changed our feelings, as we heard that cheering cry,
"Three miles to camp! three miles to camp!"
How the word ran down the column,
Cheering up the sad and solemn;
Soon came rest, for quickly passed the three miles to camp.

So, though gloomy all around us, now the war-clouds seem to lower,
Peace may not be so far distant: this may be the darkest hour.
If a message from the future, like that horseman, could but come,
It might cheer us now with promise of but three months yet to home,
Three months to home! three months to home!
Pass the word along the column,
Cheering up the sad and solemn;
Hardships some time will be o'er, and we'll be at home.

That night we camped at about 9 o'clock, and the night was too cold to let us sleep any; but there were plenty of rails, and we made them keep us warm, instead of the blankets left behind. Next morning, April 15th, reveille came at 4:30; and scarcely time enough was allowed us to boil our coffee, to say nothing of drinking it, before we were again on the move. By 8 o'clock, there began to be some resistance from a party of rebels in front; and from that time till about four in the afternoon, there was almost ceaseless skirmishing.

At 9 o'clock, our regiment being at the head of the column, and having come pretty close upon the advance-guard of cavalry, we suddenly found ourselves in direct range of a rebel battery, which at once opened upon us. Instantly there was an uproar. The shells came tearing through the trees; and there were hasty and contradictory orders, from the front and rear, to advance, and to clear the way for the artillery. For an instant there was confusion; and then the voice of the Major commanding, was heard amid the roar. "Left file," he shouted; and we left filed—that is to say, we turned off hastily to the left from the road, and attempted to find shelter behind a slight ridge of land, from the more direct and point-blank range of the masked battery.

In a few minutes we were ordered across to the other side of the road, and posted behind the same ridge, but at the right and front of the battery, we were to support. From this movement arose, for a day or two, a faint report that "the 33d Iowa ran at Poison Springs;" but the lie was so utterly baseless, it never spread much beyond the few cowardly skulkers from other regiments, who tried to set it going. The 33d Iowa did not run, did not retreat, did not break in confusion, and did not do any more nor less, than any sensible regiment would do, under similar circumstances.

For about an hour and a half there was a very brisk artillery combat; but the rebel shells went either to our left, or through the tree-tops above us. Meanwhile our skirmishers were deployed on the right front, and were gradually advancing across the open field where, behind a thicket, the rebel battery was masked. General Rice had ordered the cavalry to flank the rebels on our right, but for some cause they failed to come up. Had they executed the movement properly, or even had our line of skirmishers been doubled and pushed forward, the battery must have been captured. As it was, our main line lay there and waited, while the artillery-fire grew heavier, then gradually diminished, and finally ceased. The only casualty in our regiment was one man shot through the hand, by the accidental discharge of his gun.

At 10:30 A. M. the rebels had retreated, and we resumed the advance. Our regiment remained at the head of the column. A small squad of cavalry preceded us, but whenever there was any particular danger ahead, they regularly fell to the rear. No blame could attach to the men themselves for this, for they were the same who fought gloriously on greater fields; but their commander on this expedition seemed to us to be contemptibly worthless.

The day wore slowly on. Most of the time our way led through heavy timber. The skirmishing in front was so incessant that a ten-minute's silence, as once in a while occurred, seemed more noticeable and significant than the accustomed popping of the musketry. At frequent intervals the regiment was obliged to change formation, and march through the woods alternately in column, line of battle, column by company or platoons, or otherwise, as the circumstances seemed to demand. This made the advance additionally fatiguing. Having no object but to hinder and annoy us as much as possible, the rebels were very bold. At one time, while General Rice was riding with his staff at the head of our regiment, a rebel on horseback dashed down toward us, into plain view, and sent a bullet so close to the General that he and all his staff involuntarily "bobbed," and then the daring horseman dashed away again. As we neared Camden, the rebels made less and less resistance, and finally none at all. About a mile and a half from town we were ordered into camp, while other regiments went on; but in a few minutes the order was changed, and we marched into town.

Now was the glory of the cavalry. All along the way, so far, they had been willing to go in the rear occasionally; now they came rushing valiantly past us, rich with the forage of a country where no Union troops had ever been before, and charging furiously on as if they were taking the city — though the fact was that two companies of Infantry had been there some time before them. From their performances on this 15th of April, arose most of our opinion derogatory to the name of cavalry.

At about 6:30 P. M., we began to enter the town, in the western suburbs. The neat white houses, and the general air of the place rather pleased us; and there seemed to be a lurking impression that we would stay there a while. Rumors had been in circulation, given with all the usual definiteness and authority, that General Rice with our brigade was to remain as garrison of the place, and that this was why we, and not others, were sent on in advance of the main column. It was a long and uncomfortable walk, fatigued as we were, to wind through the streets and past the frowning fort — which made us glad the rebels had concluded to evacuate — and then out to a desolate, barren place, a half-mile or more from town, where neither wood nor water was convenient; but we struggled through it at last, and long after dark tumbled down to sleep, as best we might after the fatigues of such a day.

There are always some who, weak and tired as they may be during the day's march, even compelled to "give out" and wait for an ambulance to carry them, no sooner reach camp than they seem to have strength and life enough to ransack all the neighboring country in search of forage; and these now found means before morning to gather many a ham and pound of sugar, and pone of corn-bread, in most cases bought at a very small expenditure of legal tender. Never having seen any "green-backs" before, the people were totally ignorant of the relation they bore to customary prices, and some were quite dubious about receiving them at all; but small was the difference to us, whether they took them or not, if only we got what eatables we wanted. So here we were now in Camden, after a march much harder than any other we had experienced, with the exception of one or two days of the march from Helena; and if nothing worse had followed, we should long have looked back with feelings of no pleasant remembrance to this part of our Camden expedition.

CHAPTER XI.

THE RETREAT FROM CAMDEN.

Arrived in Camden, the march was nominally suspended; but there came little rest for us. We had to move camp some where nearly every day we were there; but in justice to our commander it should be remarked that we got a better camp each time. Since leaving Little Rock there had been no soap issued to the men, and therefore there had been almost no chance for properly washing clothes. Soap even for faces and hands, had been of unparalleled scarcity. Of course, as soon as we had rest now, and soap issued, there came unwonted activity in the laundry department. Every brook was a tub, every bush a clothes-horse, and almost every man a washer-woman. On the 18th, from some whim of the Major, or some high officer, we had parade for the first time since the expedition commenced; and a ragged affair it was. The dress-coats had been left behind, with the sashes and other extra paraphernalia of camp; and the blouses and pants we wore were almost fluttering to the wind in rags. Our band had dwindled down to two or three ragged drummers, and as many fifers who had lost their fifes; and the principal musician had a sore heel, so he paraded up and down the line with one bare foot and one shoe on. Altogether, it was a very ragged affair, and came probably as near an *un*-dress parade as the army regulations ever contemplated. Fine feathers may make fine birds, but a hard march is "death on style."

A forage-train of about a hundred wagons, with but a small escort, was sent out west from town on the morning of the 18th. It had gone out about as far as Poison Springs, or Washington Cross-Roads—the place where the artillery-duel occurred on the 15th—when it was attacked by an overwhelming force of the enemy, and after a fierce and bloody resistance was captured. There was a heavy loss of killed and wounded; but both white and black soldiers kept straggling back to town for two or three days afterward, so the total of casualties was not known. It was afterward learned that a number of the Union soldiers killed there, had been scalped by the rebels. Only one or two of our regiment were with the train, and they escaped uninjured. There was loud complaint of the culpable blunder, of sending out such a train, under such circumstances, with so small a guard; but opinion varied widely as to the responsibility of the catastrophe.

Because we had been delayed on the march beyond the calculated time, or because the supply-train, under command of Lieutenant-Colonel Mackey, ordered from Little Rock, by another route, after we started, was behind its time for arrival, we were now almost out of rations. Meat could be obtained, but hard-tack grew more rare and valuable, with each succeeding day. A small, steam-mill in town, was kept running at all hours of the day and night, grinding corn, but it was by no means large enough to supply the demand. Portable iron hand-mills were put up, and relays of four hungry men, at a time, kept them constantly in motion. Corn was issued instead of other food, which was not to be had; and one day our regularly-issued ration was four ears of corn per man.

On the evening of the 20th of April, the supply-train came in. We were heartily glad to welcome our colonel, and the recruits who came with him; but the greatest joy was over the "good old mail" which came with the train, and was distributed that evening. It was the first word we had heard from home or civilization, since the march began. Little could the writers of those letters imagine, how eagerly the envelopes were torn open, or how dear and precious the words of love and hope, from home, seemed to us, there in the enemy's country, and so long cut off from even the comforts of a camp. Welcome and prized as letters always were, they had never been so much so as now; and few of us can look back to those old days, without remembering "the good old mail we got at Camden."

Next day came such a scratching of pens on paper as was never before known in our regiment. There was word that the train would start back to Little Rock in a day or so, and take a mail with it; and so all the long letters we had been gradually writing since the march commenced, were now closed, and new ones written, and a very large amount of mail matter was started for the dear ones at home. Alas! it never arrived! The disaster at Mark's Mills, a few days later, resulted not only in the capture of some of our own comrades, among others, with the train, but in the loss of all that heavy mail. Doubtless the rebels "had a good time" in reading over the words of love and hope, or the expressions of our opinions as to the situation. Well, "turn about is fair play;" and we remembered the Yazoo Pass, where, without any undue foraging on our part, so many old letters and other documents of the "skedaddling" rebel citizens had fallen into our hands.

Company C, of our regiment, was detailed as part of the provost-guard in town. The orders concerning passes were very strict. In fact, a man without shoulder-straps could hardly get a pass at all; and the result of course was that the men went to town without passes, and didn't experience very much difficulty about it either. It is hard for a soldier to yield strict obedience always to the letter and spirit of an order which is plainly unnecessary and unjust, when he knows well enough that he may disregard it with perfect impunity. Some there were, indeed, to whom the mere fact of an order was law and penalty enough, and who made it a point of honor never to transgress it in any way; but we always noticed that these were the very men who could generally get the least favors of any, while the reckless fellows, who cared for orders no further than they feared the consequences, could be out of camp without leave and around town half the time, and be none the worse off for that. At least, if such was not the actual fact, it was certainly the general impression.

Saturday, the 23d, passed with the usual quiet and listlessness, until about a quarter after four in the afternoon, when there was suddenly heard a very brisk cannonading near a bridge, not far from town, which our picket-line was guarding. In a few minutes we were ordered into line. Men were left in camp to pack up the things, and the regiment formed hastily and marched over toward the fort. But by this time the firing had ceased; and in a few minutes we returned to camp, with orders to be ready to leave at a moment's notice. This is no uncommon order in the army, but some times it amounts to one thing, and some times to another. Oftenest, perhaps, it signifies that we would best lay in needful supplies of postage-stamps and tobacco, for we may start to-morrow; but at this particular time it meant just what it said. We knew that well enough; for there was a general feeling among us that we were "in a tight place," and might have some trouble in getting out. So our personal equipments and possessions were hastily packed and strapped, and the few cooking materials slung together and piled in readiness to be loaded into the wagons; and then came the wearisome, listless sitting around, and waiting for the orders which were all the time expected. None came, however; and we tumbled down to sleep that night, and stood "at arms" after an early reveille next morning, and then settled back into the uncertain rest of camp. The cannonading which had so suddenly come and gone, appeared to be either a disproportionately heavy, though unsuccessful, attack on the small force defending the bridge, or an exaggerated feint to cover the attack on our train at Mark's Mills. Either way, it was a strange little affair; but the latter view seemed most probable.

The arrival of Lieutenant-Colonel Mackey had of course displaced Major Gibson from command of the regiment. Whatever the general opinion of the military capacity he displayed may have been, he was certainly esteemed and respected as a man. Coming to the conclusion that he could serve the country better as a citizen than as a soldier, he had tendered his resignation, which was immediately accepted, and had started for home with the train from Camden. Captured with that, he was taken to Texas, and suffered much hardship before being finally released. One or two private soldiers of our regiment were captured at the same time, and died in a rebel prison.

The night of the 25th came with as much quiet as usual; there were no signs of any movement; but there seemed to be a strange feeling among us—a kind of presentiment—that "some thing was going to happen." Causeless as it might have been, it was so strong that some of us, after going to bed and lying restless for some time, finally got up and packed our things and made ready to move. It was not much too soon. About 11 o'clock the acting-adjutant, Lieutenant Pearce, came round and silently waked the regiment with the order to immediately make ready to leave. Perhaps no order was ever executed more quickly or quietly. In a few moments we were on the march, in the darkness of the Summer night.

Before long the word passed round that the cavalry had been sent out to Mark's Mills, and we were moving to take their place on guard. Reaching an open place in the brush some two miles south of town, we spread ourselves down to sleep for the rest of the night. At sun-rise next morning without reveille, or any thing else whatever, to waken us, the whole regiment simultaneously rose, shook and rolled up blankets, and prepared for the day. It was a strange coincidence of thought and feeling, springing from a common knowledge of a common danger. Our duty on the 26th was merely to remain near the line of arms. Toward noon there came up word from town that preparations were making for a hasty retreat. Wagons, tents, mess-chests, cooking utensils, hard-tack and meat, were destroyed by the quantity. Box after box of crackers were burned, which would have been better distributed to the soldiers who soon were in need of them. About 2 o'clock a couple of wagons brought up our rations, and their scanty amount was divided among us. Some companies, for some cause, received much more per man than others. Some men drew but just two crackers, with a small amount of meal, some meat, and coffee, for the full supply that was to last them till we reached Little Rock; and many had not more than two crackers and a half-pint of meal. A few were fortunate enough to get their meal baked up into corn-cakes at houses near, before we started, but the rest had to cook it themselves, as best they might, along the road.

It was evidently supposed that the rebels were so near, they would speedily hear of our movements; and the intention was to give them no warning of our retreat. So we had tattoo on the drums that night, with all the noise they could make; and an hour after that, when the bass drum should sound the "taps" at 9 o'clock, the regiment was to silently fall into line, and move off without further orders. This hour of waiting was a long one. Seated on the grassy slope, we speculated upon the strange appearance of circumstances, and forecasted trouble for the future. This was evidently to be a forced retreat, and in no encouraging way; but we could only obey orders, and be cheerful, and so we tried to do. Nine o'clock came at last; the bass drum sounded the "taps" with unearthly noise; and the regiment fell silently into line, and over the soft grass, moved noiselessly away. There was an enforced halt at the pontoon across the river; and here the woolen blankets began to come out of the knapsacks. It would never do to leave them for the rebels, and so most of them were cut up and destroyed; but of those that were then and afterward thrown away, the artillery-men, who came after us, and who, of course, rode most of the time on their guns and caissons, gathered up a great many, which they sold at a big profit, when we reached Little Rock again. So artillery-men, like other folks, make money some times from the calamities of their companions.

For about three miles from the pontoon-crossing, the road lay in such direction, as to be fully commanded by a battery, near where we had camped the night previous; and over this road our commanding-officers passed with us anxiously, fearing lest the rebels, who were known to be marching close upon us, might reach that battery in time to bring a few guns to bear, and so cut off our retreat. Most of the men, however, knew nothing of this, and therefore passed over the ground, as quiet and careless as usual. The event proved that the rebels were farther behind than was supposed, and that they really did not reach the river, till some time the next evening. About two o'clock in the night, the dangerous three miles having been passed over, we overtook that part of the column which had crossed the river before us. Here came a halt; and without any orders, (a most remarkable thing for soldiers), every body tumbled down on the ground to sleep. There was the most perfect equality and democracy, we had ever seen in the army. The officers had no "sleeping utensils" with them, and therefore, had to lie down as they were. General Rice was fortunate enough to have a cloak to lie on. He made a pillow of the bodies of one or two sleepy soldiers, who happened to be near him. One of the men happened to awake about 4 o'clock, and in moving a little, he almost stumbled over our division-commander, stretched upon the bare ground, with his feet to the fire, and looking like any other Dutchman.

The next day, the 27th of April, was clear and warm. Our loads were very heavy, and the march was very hard. No attack was as yet made in the rear, and hence grew rumors that the rebels had got around between us and Little Rock. Signs enough of the precipitation of our retreat appeared in the constant succession of shreds of clothing, pieces of knapsacks, and other fragments, which fatigue compelled our men to throw away. Next morning, Thursday, reveille was sounded with the bugles at five; and in twenty-six minutes from that time—before we could possibly make coffee and drink it—the march re-commenced. Never before had we seen such haste when a whole column was moving. Marching as fast as we could under the circumstances, we reached the well-built and pleasant looking little town of Princeton, about 1 o'clock, and after considerable delay went into camp in an old corn-field.

Rumors so various and contradictory that one could hardly put the least faith in any of them, were now flying thick among us. The most general belief, however, proved in the end to be the correct one—that the train sent out from Camden had been captured, the prisoners sent to Texas, and the wounded taken to Mt. Elba, a settlement not many miles distant, where the inhabitants were treating them kindly, and taking good care of them. One or two men who had fortunately escaped from the disaster at Mark's Mills, and had wandered through the wood for two or three days, living as best they might, now found and joined us.

For a few miles north from Princeton the road lay through the country which reminded us all of Iowa. No similarity of the kind we had ever noticed in the South, was more striking; but for one great difference we were proud and thankful—that the groves and prairies of Iowa had never trembled to the tread of hostile soldiers. About noon of Friday it commenced raining; and before night the mud was very bad. The rebels were now coming close upon us, and occasional cannonading in the rear was heard during the afternoon. Every night since leaving Camden we had camped in a corn-field, and this night was no exception; but the corn-field here was lower, wetter and more comfortless than ever. Nothing dry could be found to lie on, and there was no shelter from the soaking rain. For two or three days and nights we had had little of sleep and less of food; but bad as circumstances seemed, there was yet worse to come.

We contrived some way to find a little hard-tack and beef for supper, but the scanty meal was hardly done when our regiment was ordered back to the rear, where heavy skirmishing was now going on. Gloomily we gathered up our things, and tramped wearily back through the mud and water in the almost utter darkness; but before we could reach the rear outposts the skirmishing had ceased, and we were then distributed by companies as a kind of extra picket. During the greater part of the night it rained heavily. Even if we had not been on duty, there was no dry place to lie down; and if there had been, the rain was too cold a covering. So, wearily and cheerlessly passed another night, fit prelude for the bloody morrow.

CHAPTER XII.

THE BATTLE OF JENKINS' FERRY.

The morning of April 30, 1864, was a gloomy one for our little army; and the exceedingly unpleasant weather was but an unimportant item among so much else that was disagreeable. Worn down as we were with fatigue, fasting and loss of sleep, we saw ourselves now almost surrounded by an evidently overwhelming force of the enemy, who certainly had good reasons to expect a full and easy triumph. But "the race is not to the swift, nor the battle to the strong."

Early in the morning our regiment came back from the rear out-post where we had passed the preceding night on duty, to a place some half a mile nearer the river than the corn-field previously mentioned. Soon the battle commenced, with a heavy musketry-fire in the rear. The rebels had swung their long lines of regiment after regiment around upon the hights, which described some thing like a semi-circle around that part of the swampy and heavily-timbered river-bottom where we lay; and they were now closing in to press us, unprepared, to the brink of the river, where their overwhelming numbers seemed to insure our total rout and capture. Almost immediately at the commencement of the battle our regiment was ordered back to the thickest of it, and was soon part of that gallant line of defense which for seven mortal hours, by the pure force and energy of courage in desperation, repulsed every charge of the surprised and maddened foe, whose doubled ranks bore heavily down upon the thin line which we only could bring to oppose them.

The conflict was terrible to experience, but brief to tell. Seven mortal hours, with such fierce vigor and determination that the fire of musketry became one undistinguishable and unbroken roar. Charge after charge was made by the yelling rebels, only to be broken upon our line, or if possibly succeeding for a moment, to give way at last to a charge of still deeper and more deadly determination from our own brave men. The field presented little of advantage to friend or foe. A heavily-timbered bottom, swampy at best, and now so covered with water that a foot could not rest on land alone, it would have been under any other circumstances, deemed impassable.

The battle had not long continued before a dense cloud of powder-smoke settled so closely down, that at a few feet distant, nothing was distinguishable. It seemed now almost impossible to fire otherwise than at random. The rebels did, indeed, mostly fire too high or to low. Had they aimed with any thing like the usual accuracy, few of us could have escaped. But our men, with that individual thought and action, which makes the term "thinking bayonets" more appropriate to Western troops, than to any others, soon learned to stoop down, and look under the smoke sufficiently to discover the precise position of the rebel masses; and then a horizontal fire at the level of the breast, could not fail to hit its mark, unless a tree stood in the way. The crowded and more than double formation of rebel lines, must have suffered a dreadful slaughter.

Our own ranks, too, were badly thinned. Many had already fallen, both officers and men, when Colonel Mackey, riding along the line and urging to continued action, had his arm shattered by a musket-ball, and was compelled to leave the field. Concealing the loss as much as possible from the regiment, Major Boydston assumed command, and gave all his energies to the protracted conflict. Of the more severely wounded, some were borne from the field, but most had to remain unheeded. The living were too busy to attend the dead. It is hard to see a dear friend and comrade shot down by your side, and hear his piteous cries for help, and be unable to stop even to put a canteen of water to his lips, but to leave him like a dog to die as he fell, unheeded in the din and carnage of the battle; yet so it was, then. Thank God! that day is past.

The battle of Jenkins' Ferry, was one of musketry alone. The rebels brought one battery to bear upon us, and fired three or four shots from it; but the 29th Iowa and 2d Kansas colored infantry, charged upon it, and captured its guns. A battery of our own was posted at the corner of the previously mentioned corn-field, to be opened on the rebels, if they should drive our line back too far; but it was not found necessary to fire a single shot from it. While the battle was going on in the rear, our non-combatant forces were not idle. All of the train and stores that could be saved, were sent across the river, on the pontoon that had been laid; and the pontoon-wagons, and large quantities of stores were broken, scattered and destroyed. In this moving of the train, mostly at night, over an almost impassable road, was but another example of the additional power men acquire from sheer desperation.

Such a conflict as this, in the swamps and rain, could not last forever. About two o'clock in the afternoon, the day was won. Desperate courage had conquered numbers and power. The rebels abandoned the field, all their dead and wounded, and as we afterward learned, fell back in such haste and confusion, that one of their own batteries was by accident, turned upon them—the echo of whose suicidal shells was not unwelcome to our ears. Few and exhausted as we were, retreat also, was our only hope of safety. Leaving dead and wounded on the field, but with men to care for them, our forces, victorious, yet sad, withdrew toward the river, and resumed the interrupted march; and as the last straggling company crossed the swollen stream, the pontoon was cut away, and the Saline was a temporary line of separation between us and the foe. The loss of our regiment in the battle was: killed on the field—eight; wounded—one hundred and thirteen; missing—twelve; total—one hundred and twenty-three. The names of killed, wounded and prisoners, will be found appropriately marked in the Roll of the Regiment, in the Appendix.

CHAPTER XIII.

LITTLE ROCK AGAIN.

On the south side of the Saline, the mud was as bad as possible; on the north side it was as much worse than that, as that was worse than ordinary. Crossing the river, we found ourselves in a slough, which was in places waist-deep; and in which we waded, rather than walked, for some three miles. Teams stuck, and were abandoned. One wagon contained a half-dozen negro babies, of assorted sizes, belonging to the colored Americans gathered to us since we started, which had been left there, stuck in the slough, drawn there by the feeblest of all possible mules, that was just executing his last drowning kick as we waded by. One negro woman, as was told by many who said they witnessed the incident, having carried her baby as long as she felt able, threw it away and left it, as a soldier would his knapsack. What became of the child can not be told; but probably it was not the only one abandoned.

About three miles from the river we came to land again, and went into camp, in the midst of a steady rain; but before long the clouds turned their dry side toward us, and the rousing camp-fires made a show of comfort. There was rest now, in prospect, but little food. Many of the men's rations were entirely exhausted, and all were nearly so; but there was no help for us till we reached Little Rock. Sleep instead of food will do very well, if one can but get it; and we were weary and exhausted enough to try it. At a little after mid-night, however, the order came, to burn our wagons and most of our equipage, and be ready to march at 4 o'clock in the morning. We privates were not so much interested in the wagons just then, but the officers had all their fine clothes in them; so there came a sudden change of garments, to save the best from burning; and men who had laid down ragged and dirty at dark were seen at day-light finely dressed in glossy coats with shining buttons, but hungry and tired as ever. Mess-chests, company-boxes, &c., made excellent fuel; and by their blaze the coffee was boiled and the poor pretense of breakfast eaten.

"The 1st of May is moving day." At 4 o'clock in the morning we were moving. Our division was in the front, and our regiment, train-guard. There was a mile or two of marching through mud-holes, and then came the mud in earnest. A pine swamp of four miles' width, in the worst possible condition naturally, and now cut up into almost unfathomable softness by the wagons and artillery that had already crossed it, lay between us and solid land again. Oh! the interminable teams in that dreary swamp! Driven to the last extreme of haste by the imperative necessity for food, and expecting every minute to hear the guns of the once repulsed, but still overwhelming enemy, open upon our rear, there we were compelled to wait and linger, while the long train of wagons would stick in the mud, and the mules would flounder in the mire. One of the most wearisome and vexatious things in the world is compulsory delay; and here we had it under the most disagreeable circumstances. Many as were the wagons that had been destroyed, the train still stretched out apparently two or three miles. Our duty as train-guard that day, was to cut down all the young pine trees near, bring them on our backs to that deepest part of the mire, which was called the road, and so build corduroy across most of the swamp. When a wagon stuck—and all the wagons were constantly sticking—every endeavor was made to raise it out of the mud and get it moving again. If all means failed, the mules were unhitched, and the wagon broken and burned; and so all over the swamp, near the road, were burning wagons and their scattered contents. If the cartridges that were sown that day should bear fruit even sixty-fold, there would never be peace any more. Whenever a wagon was fired, most or all of its contents were thrown into the water bunches and elsewhere; but still the occasional explosions of powder, cartridges, &c., lent variety without beauty to the scene.

At last the four miles wore away, and between one and two P. M. we came to land again. From this time until dark, the march went fast and steadily. All day the weather had been clear and pleasant; but perhaps no one had thought of its being Sunday. Notwithstanding all the rumors and fears, the rebels made no further demonstrations. One good trial had been enough for them; and certainly we were as well pleased as ever Jeff. Davis was to be "let alone." Some where near dark there came a halt, with the usual appearances of going into camp. An open field in front of us was aglow along one side with fires that looked like the camp-fires of regiments that had marched in the advance. Worn and weary as we were, and faint from the loss of food and sleep, the idea of camping for the night, seemed as pleasant as coming home might be at some other time. But there was to be no rest. The halt was only caused by another series of mud-holes, and the fires had been kindled as lights along the road.

And all that night the march continued, with no stop but what the mud enforced, till four o'clock next morning. The road was all the way through timber; and details of cavalry kindled and kept up continuous fires, till through the whole forest ran a sinuous line of fitful flames. It was a strange, wild time. We were now almost at the limits of human powers of endurance. Nature will be revenged at last, for there is a point where even her forbearance ceases. All through the night there came frequent little halts of a moment or two, caused by some wagon sticking in a mud-hole; and at every such halt, the instant we ceased moving we were asleep. Many did not feel safe to stop thus, without asking some comrade to be sure and wake them when the start was made; and many actually slept while marching.

Morning came at last, but brought no rest. Having no thing to eat, we did not need to halt for breakfast or dinner; and so we steadily marched on. Still the reports came that the rebels were between us and Little Rock. We had been hungry for some time, but now began to actually suffer for want of food. One man paid a comrade two dollars for a single hard-tack, and another traded a silver watch for two of them. That afternoon, between three and four o'clock, we came out upon the Benton road, and then knew where we were; and in an hour or so we camped, this last night of the march, on the very ground where we had camped the first night of the expedition, more than a month before. How we contrasted the two nights! and how long seemed the time between them!

Kindling fires and making coffee—for this soldier's solace was not yet exhausted—we flung ourselves down to rest. In an hour or two there arose a shout in the advance, which was quickly caught up and passed down the line. The rations had come! Orders had been sent into Little Rock for food; and besides the regular issues by the Quarter-master, our comrades left in camp there, had gathered and sent out all they had, to aid us. Never were rations more speedily distributed, or "hard-tack and sow-belly" put inside of blue uniforms with greater haste. The worst was now over. The night was altogether too cold for comfort, but sleep was a necessity and came of course.

Next morning the march was renewed with better hope and vigor. We felt as if almost home. At 10:30 Fort Steele was in sight; and not even the memory of the dreary days of fatigue-duty on its walls could make it seem unwelcome. Halting now to form in better order, the prisoners captured on the march were put between closer files, the ranks all better "dressed," and the "mule brigade"—composed of the sick, weak and wounded who were unable to walk, but who on reporting to the doctor had been supplied with mules—formed in some thing like regular military style. There would undoubtedly have been a good deal of music, but the fifes and drums had been so nearly used up on the campaign, the pounding was hardly as lively as usual.

Marching down through town on the old, familiar streets, and past General Steele's head-quarters, we finally reached our own old camp before noon. Oh! it was joy to be there again! It seemed like home. The welcomes of the comrades who had been left there were warm and cordial; but some thing to eat was the first, and the mail the second, great object of attention. Every thing eatable disappeared like grass before an army of locusts; and it seemed almost strange to be where we could get plenty to eat again. Then came the rest, which took a good while. It seemed almost dream-like to be back there in our old camp—almost too good to be true. We were glad and thankful. Colonel Mackley being disabled, Captain Boydston was temporarily in command of the regiment—a duty of which the chief visible point was to hold parade.

And so was ended the Camden Expedition. Considering the object in primary view, it was a failure; and it narrowly escaped ending in a terrible defeat. But if examples of stern and determined endurance, of desperate courage successfully resisting the force of overwhelming numbers, of faithful attempts to obey orders, and cheerful fortitude in braving disaster, are worthy of remembrance, our memories of the Camden Expedition need not be less proud than terrible.

CHAPTER XIV.

CAMP AND GARRISON.

Soon after our return to Little Rock, Captain Lofland, of Company D, having been promoted to lieutenant-colonel, assumed command of the regiment. Renewed attention was now paid to drill and discipline, and the result was marked improvement. But it was hard for us, after so much soldiering as we had tried, to see the practical benefit of so much daily drill; and the more experience we had, the stronger grew our conviction that half the drilling in the army is of no use so far as fighting is concerned, but that it serves only to make appearances better on reviews and other dress occasions. Drill in loading and firing, and in some of the more common and necessary evolutions, is all we could ever find to be of any use in actual battle. The skirmish-drill, however, we admitted to be valuable and necessary; and more attention was now paid to it. The buglers and other musicians were put through a regular daily drill; and the non-commissioned officers were for some weeks assembled every evening for practice in the bugle signal for skirmishers.

On the 28th of May a flag of truce brought in some letters from our wounded comrades of the battle of Jenkins' Ferry, who were held as prisoners at Mt. Elba, Princeton and Camden; and letters, medicines and clothing were sent out in return. Small as the consolation was of thus hearing from imprisoned and suffering comrades, it was much better than the barbarous treatment of those who fell into rebel hands in other places. And for this amenity in warfare we believe we have to thank the rebel General Price.

Among the other improvements now undertaken in camp, our acting-adjutant, Lieutenant C. H. Sharman, Company G, commenced the preparation of an entire new set of regimental books. They were finished in about a month, and were commended by every Inspecting Officer as peculiarly neat, full and correct. During the retreat from Camden the most of our regimental- and company-records had been burned among the other luggage, by order of the commanding-general; and it was therefore difficult afterward, to make all the accounts come out square.

The monotony of camp- and garrison-duty, picket and fatigue, picket and fatigue, over and again, and that continually, was interrupted by little more than frequent walks around town. There were of course details occasionally made for guards to accompany boats carrying provisions to Fort Smith, Pine Bluffs and elsewhere; and on some of these trips there were stirring times, when a squad of rebels would attack the boat. Every time a boat went out from Little Rock, before it returned, reports would come of its having been attacked, captured, sunk, &c.; but generally there would be little truth in them. On one occasion, however, one man of our regiment was mortally wounded during an attack on a boat between Little Rock and Fort Smith.

In the afternoon of Monday, June 6th, there was a grand review of our division, before Major-General Sickles, then on his tour as General Inspecting Officer; and on the 20th, our brigade was reviewed by Colonel Marcy, of the Regular Army.

Reviews and Inspections seemed now to be about the only occupation of general officers. On these occasions the field-music of the brigade was usually massed at the head of the column, so as to supply the whole four regiments together. One advantage of this was that there was no mixing up of time by different bands; but there was the disadvantage that not even the racket of ten or twenty fifes, fifteen or twenty snare-drums, and two or three bass-drums could all the time be heard by the whole brigade.

Toward the last of June, the ceremony of brigade-guard-mounting was instituted. It was held on the open space, between us and the camp of the 29th, where formerly stood the cabins of the 3d Iowa battery. The bands of the brigade took turns in furnishing the music. On the 3d of July our former Major, H. D. Gibson, who, on his way home from Camden had been captured at Mark's Mills, and had suffered great hardships during his captivity at Tyler, Texas, arrived in camp, clad in a poor suit of butternut homespun, with an old straw hat and not the best foot-gear in the world, and looking very unlike the portly and comfortable Major he was when we last saw him. Having at last succeeded in obtaining a release from the rebels, he had footed it so far toward home, and in a few weeks more he was safe in the North again.

The 4th of July this year passed very quietly. The only celebration of the day in Little Rock was that all the regiments at the post stood in arms on their color-lines, while a national salute was fired from Fort Steele. It was a tame enough affair for us who had "seen the 4th at Helena." For some cause or other, we never knew definitely what, there came now a time when we could send no letters home. The mails would leave camp as usual, but as we afterward learned, they did not leave Duvall's Bluff for a month or more. July 16th there was an alarm of attack on some of our force guarding the railroad from Little Rock to the Bluff, and a thousand men from our brigade, with a day's rations and sixty rounds of amunition were immediately sent out as re-inforcements; but they came back a little after noon, with orders to hold themselves in readiness, and were never called for again.

Next evening, the 17th, in an almost perfectly clear sky, as some of us were looking dreamily, we perceived a long and very slender line of white cloud, reaching across the sky from north-west to south-east, tracing the side of a shield of very nearly the usual shape. Of course it had to be made an "omen" in some way; and so every man drew his own inferences or forebodings.

On the 21st of July, the news reached us of the death of General Samuel A. Rice, at his residence in Iowa, from wounds received at the battle of Jenkins' Ferry. Half-hour-guns were fired from Fort Steele during the day, in honor of his memory.

The time still passed monotonously in garrison-duty. Occasionally, by way of variety, some of the officers would get up a "grand rat-ification meeting" by prying up the floors of their tents, upon which whole droves of rats would immediately scatter themselves promiscously over camp, to be captured and killed by the gathered braves, who, armed with sticks, would go through the contest with great military display if not much tactical order. The pay-master arrived on the 15th of August, and paid us for the past six months. On the 19th a recruiting-party, consisting of two line and several non-commissioned officers from the regiment, started for Iowa. How we almost envied them! About this time there began to be rumors that "Mr. Price" was collecting a number of his friends, to come and pay us a visit; and there was much speculation in camp as to whether he would be able to come inside of our lines if he should try it. The garrison of the place was now so reduced, we felt very doubtful of our ability to withstand a strong attack. On the 24th of the month, by the efforts of Lieutenant-Colonel Lofland, we drew entirely new arms and equipments, which at least improved the appearance of the regiment, if not its effective fighting power.

In the first days of September, the rumors of approaching attack became so strong that the almost invariable order in case of alarm was received — "Reveille at three, and stand at arms till sun-rise," to which we were by this time so accustomed that it was obeyed after the easy interpretation, by stacking arms on the color-line and then breaking ranks. But the rumors came thick and fast, and lost no thing as they came. Sunday morning at 3 o'clock our bugle sounded, and was immediately echoed all over town. The whole force was in arms and line. That night we went to bed as usual; but at 10 o'clock the "assembly" called us out, and with arms, canteens and rubber blankets we marched out to a portion of the defenses, some two miles west of camp, and then tumbled down and slept till some time the next forenoon, waiting for Mr. Price.

Monday was hot and cloudless. Tiring of that bare place on the ground, we moved a little nearer to the wood, and went hard at work putting up a shade, of posts, poles and boughs, as protection from the intense rays of the sun. Just as we got it well fixed, and were ready to rest awhile under it, the order came to move back to camp again; and so regretfully we left our woodland bower. "Locking the stable after the horse is lost," is hardly considered a wise rule of action. Now that the danger was apparently over, or so much so that we need no longer remain under arms and in the line of defenses, there came very heavy details for fatigue-parties to throw up earth-works, which, it seemed to us, ordinary common sense would never have omitted so long.

On the next day, however, these heavy details for unusual hours of labor were countermanded; the stars and stripes, which for the past two or three days, had given place to the red hospital-flag, were again run up to the top of the tall flag-staff, in front of the general hospital; and things seemed suddenly to have settled back to the *statu quo*. This quick transition from one state of affairs to the appearance of another, produced much mystification and distrust; but the facts at the bottom of it, when we learned them, were plain enough: Mr. Price had simply "passed by on the other side," and gone up toward Missouri.

Drills and parades, inspections and reviews, returned now with increased persistence, and took about all the time that picket- and fatigue-duty left unoccupied. Brigade-guard-mounting, was still the daily order. On the 23d of September, an added interest was given it, by the first appearance of our new brigade brass band—usually styled among us "Mein Bender's Band," as General Salomon called it—from Milwaukee, Wisconsin. This band was composed of some fifteen or twenty musicians, nearly all Germans. It discoursed really excellent music, and was a credit to the brigade. No dress occasion was complete without them; and when not on public-duty, they were kept very busy in serenading different officers around town. On the 25th of the month, for the sake of still higher "style," and perhaps, also, for the sake of giving the general and field officers some thing to attend to, division-guard-mounting was instituted. This was a somewhat imposing display. All the guard-details of our whole division, and all the officers not on duty at the time, had to attend in full uniform; and the whole was a spectacle with much of the "pomp and circumstance" about it. There was usually a large number of spectators, both soldiers and citizens; and even the commanding-general occasionally came out to look on.

News still came some times from the outside world. On the 4th of October, one hundred guns were fired, from the five different forts around town, in honor of Sheridan's great victory in the Shenandoah Valley. On the 8th, further news came of a tremendous victory gained by General Grant, in which he was said to have captured twenty-five hundred prisoners and one hundred guns. This, however, seemed then, as it afterward proved to be, altogether too good to be true. Accompanying all these good reports, but more real than they, Colonel Mackey returned to the regiment, from an absence of three or four months in Iowa, with his wounded arm so nearly well, as to allow of his assuming his command.

Preparations were now commenced toward fitting the camp for Winter. The officers began building new cabins, and the streets were all changed and cleared. Among the other improvements, perhaps, the three new brass drums received for the band, are worth a mention. Company G contributed forty dollars to buy a brass drum for "Tommy," in whose drumming they had well-merited pride; and not to be outshone entirely, the drummer of Company H, and "Johnny" of Company I, bought new drums at their own expense. These, of course, added much to the noise and rattle of the "music." There were expectations now of our remaining in quarters for the Winter; and circumstances certainly seemed to indicate it. But "all signs fail in a dry time;" and there is no dependance to be placed on them in the army. The monotony was soon broken. Of course, if there was any thing to be done, the 33d was the regiment to do it; and soon the unwelcome order came for a move.

CHAPTER XV.

TO FORT SMITH AND BACK.

On Sunday, October 30, 1864, our regiment, with a section of the 3d Iowa battery, started out as escort of a train of supplies for Fort Smith. Nothing very special occurred at the commencement of this march. We were used to the business, and knew by this time "how to make the best of it." For the first night we camped in the wood about eight miles from town; the second night, at the Palaime Bayou; the third night, on the Arkansas river, some three miles from the Cadron, where we had to lie over one day to wait for the train to cross the little river. Here some sport and excitement were caused by a chase after half-wild horses on the river bottom. Several of them were finally lassoed.

Not far from noon the 4th of November, we entered Lewisburg, and camped in the outer edge of the little town. The night was cold, with a severe frost; and this made the hard ground a rather cold bed for us. Next day we passed through some country which looked very much like Iowa—a similarity sure to be noticed—but the likeness soon ceased. About five miles from Lewisburg we came upon the Carroll farm—the largest plantation we had ever seen. Thousands of acres of fertile bottom-lands, now in total neglect, and overgrown with weeds, seemed a fit place for the "deserted village" of negro-quarters which stood at a respectful distance from the planter's door. Of course, "the ole man wuz gond, an' the niggers wuz in Texas."

On the night of the 5th, we camped some eleven miles west of Lewisburg. Just in advance of us was a company of colored infantry, and beyond them a part of the 2d Arkansas Infantry, who were to go with us the rest of the way. This camp of the 2d Arkansas was the queerest thing in the military line in all our experience. The members of the regiment had formerly lived some where in this part of the State; and they were now moving all their wives, children, stock, furniture, wagons, and other property, to Fort Smith. Every thing among them seemed to us to be in promiscuous confusion. We were not accustomed to the sight of soldiers among their families. It must have been hard for women and children to take such a march at such a time, and under those circumstances; but there were many among them who at the hands of the fiends of rebel guerrillas, their own neighbor's family, had suffered wrongs and cruelties compared with which, these hardships were as nothing. After talking some time with them, and with other Southerners who were, and had always been truly loyal, we frequently declared to ourselves that so long as our dear ones at home were safe and comfortable, we would grumble no more — that we knew no thing of the hardships and troubles of the war.

During this halt dispatches were received, announcing the defeat of Price and his rebels in Missouri, and their scattered retreat toward the Arkansas river. Some doubt was entertained of the expediency of our passing very near his flying columns; and a delay of one day in our march was therefore attributed to this cause. On the 7th, starting on again, we made about fourteen miles, and camped for the night around the residence of a Mr. Potts, an arrant old rebel. A large white house, with big barns and granaries, commanding a near view of the abrupt and imposing "Carrion-Crow Mountain," it would have been a good enough home for a much better man. Foraging was prohibited, but not prevented, and the secesh proprietor of the premises unwillingly contributed to the Union army enough to make us two pretty good meals, at least, and very probably suffered the loss of more.

All along the road, the country hereabouts seemed to be good, and well settled. The women and children appeared to be all gathered at the neighbors' houses to look at us, while the men were out in the woods "bushwhacking." There was considerable apprehension among us of trouble with these bushwhackers, and frequent reports came of our having been fired into from the sides of the road; but most or all of these stories, when traced up, were found to start from some wagon-master or train-teamster.

About 1:30 P. M., of November 8th, we camped in a field on the Illinois bayou, three miles from Russellville. In a little while a small wedge-tent was put up, rude tables constructed under it, and the polls opened for election. We felt that on this day the great conflict was to be decided, and we did our duty as we could. That night it rained hard, and did not stop till it turned cold next morning. This made a very uncomfortable time. A warm rain, if followed by a clear, warm day, is little heeded in the army; but a soaking flood of water, followed only by clouds, cold and winds, is exceedingly unwelcome. Resuming the march, we found that the bayou, had risen several inches; and as there was no other means of crossing, we had to wade through it. The cold, raw wind, as well as the coldness of the water, spoiled all the fun of the thing, and we marched along about as cheerfully as a poor man goes to jail. That night, after a march of about fourteen miles over a very rough and rocky road, we camped in a large field on the Big Piney bayou.

Next day, the 10th, starting at about seven in the morning, as usual, we entered Clarkesville by the covered bridge over Spadra Creek at about 1:15 P. M.; halted a few minutes, and then turned back to camp on the bluff. There had been a slight skirmish near this place, between our advance-cavalry and a small squad of rebels, and one or two guerrillas were killed. All we regretted was, that any of the diabolical wretches were left alive. All along the road of late, we had seen the ruins of houses they had burned because their occupants were Union men, or were supposed to have a little money; and there were persons with us who personally knew, and told us, of the guerrillas entering such and such houses, whose ruins we passed, and torturing the inmates by burning their feet over a fire to make them give up their money. At such times, if we could have got hold of the rebel devils, we would have hewn them to pieces.

One pathetic incident occurred at Clarksville, of which Sergeant Hamsick and Commissary-Sergeant Berkey were witnesses. An old widow living near town stood looking at our little column as it entered town, and suddenly her eye fell on the countenance of her son, whom she had not seen or heard of for a long time. He was a soldier in the 2d Arkansas. After the first surprise and excitement of the meeting, she told him how the infernal bushwhackers had been at her house, and had insulted and actually beaten her, and killed an aged man living near. It is to be hoped the old lady's son was able to save her from further troubles from them.

At Clarksville we laid over for a day, and sent out a train after forage, which returned without any great supply. The 1st

Arkansas Infantry, and the 5th U. S. Colored Infantry arrived from Fort Smith as additional escort for our train; and Colonel Johnson, of the 1st, being the senior officer, assumed command. Starting out again rather early next day, we made some fourteen miles, and a little after noon approached the place that had for some days been dreaded—a narrow canyon called Horsehead Pass, which was represented as the very nest and head-quarters of all the bushwhackers in the country. A fit place for them indeed it was. For a considerable distance the road wound between the almost meeting hills, whose rugged, precipitous and wooded sides gave every opportunity of concealment and safety for a lurking foe. Fifty well-armed men here could have terribly harassed ten thousand. After the pass came the narrows, where the sides of the canyon, though not so high, were nearer together. As we entered the pass, heavy details of flankers were sent out on each side, relieved or reinforced at frequent intervals. Three or four shots were heard as we passed through the defile, but it is not fully certain whether they were fired by bushwhackers or by men of our own force who were camped in advance of us and had gone out foraging. It was of course well to use all possible precaution in such a place, but the danger proved in no wise equal to our expectations.

About 2 o'clock of Tuesday, the 15th, we entered the town of Van Buren, on the Arkansas river, and marched down to camp a mile or two below town, on the river bank. Here we laid over a day, for the train to unload, as the river was so high we could not well cross. Fort Smith was only five miles distant, and we very much wished to go there. Many did foot it the next day, for the sake of seeing the place and going "out of the United States into the Indian Territory." Thursday, the 17th, we turned our faces homeward, as going back to

Little Rock then seemed to us. Marching fourteen miles, we camped that night on the ground occupied a few nights before. It rained hard, and was very muddy and disagreeable. One who had never tried it would be astonished to see how much shelter may be made of one common rubber blanket. Suspended by stakes so as to hang in the form of an obtuse-angled roof, about three feet from the ground, it will keep two soldiers passably dry through the rainiest of nights, provided the wind doesn't blow, and the men will lie still and close together. Some shelter for us on this return trip seemed almost necessary, for the rain came down with all persistency.

The boys now seemed to have much better success in foraging than when we went the other way. Tobacco was the great staple. The supply brought with us from Little Rock, having been long ago exhausted, it may be imagined that "natural leaf" and "twist," were doublv welcome. Loads of it were foraged. The cavalry got the most, as usual; but before we reached Lewisburg, all had as much as they wanted to use.

Colonel Bowen and Mr. Gilsoate, two old men from Hempstead County, Representatives in the State Legislature, came with us to Little Rock. They were true Union men, as was apparent in every word and act, and had suffered much for their loyalty. The elder of the two, had lived in Hempstead County, most of his life; and it was intensely amusing to hear him describe and illustrate his utter ignorance of the machinery and improvements of modern civilization. A short visit to the North, a few months previous, had evidently convinced him, that there was no people on earth, like the Yankees, and that the sooner they whipped the South out, and re-settled the country, the better it would be for every body.

Having now been out of the reach of news for some time, we naturally supposed that at least, some thing must have happened in the world, since we started. We had no doubt that Lincoln was re-elected; and many were sure there would be some great news from Richmond. But in this we were disappointed. Reaching Lewisburg, which was connected by telegraph with Little Rock, we heard of Lincoln's triumph, and of Sherman's starting toward Charleston; but from Richmond came nothing remarkable. Long months after this, when the news did finally come, of the overthrow of the rebel strong-hold, it had been, as is usual with so much expected events in life, so heralded and introduced, that the reality, though vast, did not seem equal to the anticipation.

Not far from our camp, three miles west of the Cadron, we noticed a tall cotton-wood stump, about two feet in diameter, hollow, and running down several feet straight into the ground, thus conclusively showing, that the ground there, for at least that depth, was all deposited by the action of water, within the last hundred years or so. The second night of the march out from Little Rock, we had camped in and around a good, old white house, at the bridge across the Palarme. Coming back now, only two or three weeks later, we found the house had been burned; so we camped in the out-buildings and on the vacant lots. Familiar with destruction, we had never yet seen so much house-burning, as had been done on the road from Little Rock to Fort Smith.

Next morning, the 27th of November, we had reveille at three o'clock, and by dint of much hurrying, got on the move again before six. There was as yet no trace of day-light, and so we crossed the high bridge over the Palarme, by the glowing light of two large fires. It was a picturesque scene. But starting before day-light, was rather overdoing the matter; and we had to halt and wait half an hour or so for sun-rise, and then went on our way rejoicing, for this was our last day's march.

Not far from four o'clock in the afternoon, we found ourselves in sight of town. Our band met us at the pontoon-bridge; and we marched up through town with all the glory of fifes and drums, our ragged and dusty uniforms contrasting shabbily with the bright, new clothes, and paper collars of the city soldiers. But for some cause or other, there was the largest and most enthusiastic crowd gathered to see us, of all qualities and descriptions, military and civilians, that we had ever seen on the streets of Little Rock, since the city fell into our hands.

Arrived in our old camp again, we found our comrades of the last recruiting-party all returned; and the mail that had accumulated during our absence now cheered us all at once. But much inconvenience and some loss had been caused by the stay of the 47th Indiana for several days in our quarters while we were gone. The Fort Smith trip was the longest we were ever on. It had included about 360 miles of consecutive marching, but there was nothing more or worse about it than "mere common soldiering." All had stood it first-rate, and many liked it much better than remaining in camp. The health of the regiment was never better. But the more thoughtful among us noticed, and deplored, the hardening influence a march invariably has upon the finer tastes and sensibilities. It seemed to deaden our better feelings. Remaining quiet in camp for some time, our æsthetic natures seemed to live and grow, but on the march they seemed chilled and stunned by hard realities. Three months of comparative rest would not more than remedy the hardening effect of a month of marching.

CHAPTER XVI.

REST A LITTLE, AND THEN OFF AGAIN.

In camp once more, the usual routine ensued. Fatigue, picket, drill and parade were the standing order of the day, with inspection and review for variation. One evening on parade the solemnity of the occasion was materially interrupted by a couple of little boys who came out among the rest to witness the performances. Tickled most, of course, by the fifes and drums, they followed close behind them; and when the band struck up for the march down and back in front of the line, close behind them tagged the little boys, their short legs wiggling rapidly as they tried to keep up with the music. Down and up the line marched the band as usual, and down and up the line followed the boys, to the intense amusement of the regiment, and the great disgust of the principal musician, who was rallied a good deal over his new recruits.

December 24th, in the morning, a full and distinct rain-bow was visible for some minutes, though the weather was very cold. We could explain it only by supposing the frost in the air had consented to act instead of rain for this particular occasion. Major-General J. J. Reynolds was now in command of the department, and the straightening-up he made there was very perceptible. He inspected our regiment on the 20th of January, and complimented us afterward on our appearance — promising a more general inspection in quarters before many days; from which some inferred quite positively that we were still to remain in town on garrison-duty. But they were soon undeceived.

On the morning of the 21st of January, unexpected orders came for us to be ready to march immediately, with ten days' rations, blankets, and general "heavy-marching order." Most of us believed this to be the beginning of that grand "onward movement" toward Texas which all expected to come in the Spring. Next morning we left our camp again, for another "last time!" A review of the moving force took place in front of the general hospital; and at a quarter after eleven the march commenced. The column consisted of three or four regiments of infantry, with some cavalry and artillery, and was under the command of Brigadier-General Carr. The most utter and unprecedented ignorance prevailed as to our destination, or the probable length of our stay; and all sorts of conjectures were afloat concerning both questions.

The first day's march was but about eight miles, on the Pine Bluff road. Before night it commenced snowing considerably; and the ground became decidedly too cold to sleep on, with comfort. It is very easy for a healthy man to warm up an ordinary bed, by the heat of his body, but it is comparatively difficult thus to warm a whole planet. Next day, marching about ten miles, we camped for the night, on a rather good plantation, then owned by a widow lady, who was naturally very anxious to save her rails and chickens, and therefore discanted considerably upon the fact that her daughters were at school in Indiana; that her husband had been a good Union man; that the rebels had been around there several times and hung him, to punish him for his loyalty; and that at last they had hung him so much that it injured his health, and he finally died. Of course, we respected the chickens and rails.

About noon of the 25th, we entered Pine Bluff, where the Dutch rebel Marmaduke, had been so often and signally repulsed, by the gallant Clayton, and where the condensed and substantial earth-works attested the determined character of the defense, as the buildings in town, showed plainly the fierceness of the onset. Passing through the streets with but little delay, we went into camp about a mile below town. Next day we made some twelve or fourteen miles, without special incident; and on Friday following, traveled sixteen miles, passing a good, white, frame school-house—an exceedingly rare thing in Arkansas. This brought us to the settlement called Mt. Elba, on the Saline river.

Here, camped on an open field, we lay over for two days, while the cavalry pressed on toward Camden, to raise an alarm there, and cause a concentration of the rebel forces. Having nothing to do meanwhile, but to lie still and wait for their return, we sent out a forage-train, which came back well loaded with provisions. This part of the country having never before been occupied by Union troops, except in transit, there was the more left for us; and we lived on the fat of the land. On Monday the cavalry came back, and we turned our faces once more toward the North. A long and tiresome march, through rain and mud, left us for the night, on the place we had occupied the preceding Thursday; and on the next night, after a very fatiguing tramp through the mud, we found ourselves a mile and a half north-west of Pine Bluff, on the road to Little Rock.

Wednesday, February 1st, was another hard day for us, with only mud and rain instead of comfort. It is not easy to march under twenty pounds of knapsack, and twenty or twenty-five pounds of other accoutrements, even on good roads; and mud knee-deep has no tendency to help the matter. But there was no enemy now to hover in our rear, and no prospect of starvation if we did not hurry. Lying over at Rock Springs on Thursday, to wait for our train to come up, we started out again on Friday, and camped that night on the plantation of the widow Campbell, whose husband had been so injuriously hung.

Saturday, the 4th, brought us again to Little Rock, though only for a little while. When we were yet two or three miles out of town, word was brought to us, that we were under immediate orders for New Orleans. Strange as it seemed to us, to be likely to get out of Arkansas, there were many who believed the story, and more who hoped it was true. We had been seeing active service lately; though this last trip had been but easy and ordinary soldiering. All had got along exceedingly well; and the sickness among the regiment had been reduced to the minimum.

There was now for us a short period of complete rest, even the details for fatigue- and guard-duty being remitted; and in consequence, the line of the regiment on parade, had a length which reminded us of the old Camp-Tuttle-days, before sickness and battle had so reduced our numbers. Having before now, repeatedly left Little Rock "for the last time," the parting had become an old story; but this coming time was to be the last indeed. We had no special love for the old place, but having been stationed there for more than half of our term of service, it was but natural for us to feel connected with it by some ties of association. But these were soon parted, and Little Rock became only one more name in the album of our military memories.

CHAPTER XVII.

DOWN SOUTH.

Our Valentine for 1865, came one day too early, in the shape of marching orders for New Orleans. Tuesday, February 14, rose gloomy enough, and it was cloudy and chilly, when not raining, all the rest of the day. If "signs" were to be of any avail, our trip was to be a sad one. At half-past six in the morning, we bade our final adieu to the old camp where so much of our soldier-life had been passed, crossed the river on the wooden pontoon-bridge, and piled ourselves and baggage on the train for Duvall's Bluff. Every moment brought vividly to mind the contrast between our first coming to the city and this last departure from it. When we first arrived at Little Rock, it was amid the smoke of burning buildings, cars and boats. The streets were deserted, the stores were empty; and we looked upon the city as a temporary stopping-place in our march from Helena to Texas. Now it was a busy, bustling town, familiar to us as more than a year's residence could make it. Then, we marched wearily over the prairie, day by day, suffering from heat and thirst, and wondering if we should ever see happier circumstances there. Now, we rode lightly and cheerily along, with no fatigue and comparatively little comfort, passing in a few hours what had taken us toilsome days before. Then, we were in but feeble hope for the end of the rebellion, and looked upon it as a distant and intangible uncertainty. Now, we saw the end approaching, and felt sure that victory could not tarry long. We were bidding farewell to familiar scenes, but with hope brighter than ever, that before many months longer we should greet the still desired and more familiar scenes of home.

Arriving at Duvall's Bluff about noon, we waited a long while for "red tape" to furnish proper transportation, and while climbing and sliding around the muddy hills, had ample time to contrast the past and present appearance of the place. Some time in the afternoon we embarked on the steamer *Paragon*, and started down the river. To men who have been either lying in camp, working on fatigue-duty, or tramping over the heaven-forsaken pine swamps of Arkansas, so long as we had, there is a pleasing novelty in marching on a steamboat, even with all the discomforts of the manner in which soldiers are packed and stowed away.

Tying up at night for safety, we went steaming on down the river next day; and at a little before 1 P. M. came in sight of the noble Mississippi again, with feelings of gladness and welcome, and soon afterward rounded to and went ashore to camp at a little huddle of houses where a small squad of Union troops was stationed. The gun-boat *Tyler* lay here; and the sight of her brought back to memory the "bloody 4th" she helped us celebrate at Helena. Next morning, the 16th, the *Paragon* having gone up the river, we went on board the large and splendid steamer *Ben Stickney*, and went speeding southward, rejoicing in the increased room she gave us.

At noon we reached Vicksburg, the historic city. Lying up there till night, we had time to wander around and see the fortifications, and note the traces of the mighty contest. And the more we saw, the more we wondered—not th" it took

General Grant so long to take the city, but that it was ever taken. Leaving Vicksburg that night, we found ourselves on Sunday, floating down between the low, luxurious and orange-laden banks of the lower Mississippi; and at three o'clock in the afternoon of the 19th, arrived at New Orleans. Some members of the regiment had been there before; but to most of us the scenes had all the charm of novelty and of contrast with all we had left behind. As soon as the boat tied up for a few minutes to another boat lying at the levee, the fruit-women and juvenile vendors of all sorts of basket-fixings came swarming to us like the locusts of Egypt. We were all "nearly strapped;" but the oranges must be had, and in many cases the last cent went for them. The fact is, human beings in army-blue and under such circumstances, can't stand more than a certain amount of temptation.

So soon as the necessary reports could be made to head-quarters, and the necessary orders obtained, we crossed the river and landed on the Algiers side. There was considerable delay in getting all our things off the boat; and it was dark and raining when we reached the large, flat, open field, not far from the river, which was to be our camp for a few days. All sorts of rumors were current as to our further destination, but most of them tended to Mobile Bay. Every thing now seemed strange and novel. Baggage and transportation were cut down to limits that seemed exceedingly slim, even to us "old soldiers" as we almost thought ourselves. Next day, our extra clothing and other property was packed in boxes, and sent home by express, or stored in the city.

Tuesday night, February 21st, was one of the most uncomfortable times we had experienced. A heavy rain came on, flooding the low, flat ground to the depth of two or three inches, leaving us either to sleep half buried in water, or to get up and wade around till it should fall away. It was a cheerless crowd, that looked like so many drowned rats in camp next morning.

On Thursday, the 23d, marching down to the nearest landing we went on board the *Izetta*, an old side-wheel boat that looked as though she would hardly hold together to cross the river. She did, however, and more too; for she carried us up and down, here and there, forward and backward, seeking the proper landing, for some thing less than half a day. Toward night the rain commenced; and right in the midst of it, between seven and eight in the evening, we took the cars on the Ponchartrain railroad; and after a crowded ride of nearly an hour were unloaded at the wharf on the lake shore. Here was confusion, in almost utter darkness. Only those who have tried it can imagine the bustle and vexation of moving a regiment with all its baggage from the cars to a boat under such circumstances. To make it worse, there was not transportation for all of us. Three companies were put on board the little river-boat *A. G. Brown*, three more on the gulf-steamer *Alabama;* and the remaining four companies had to wait for another boat.

For our first experience on salt-water, between the lake and Navy Cove, we had smooth weather, and met with no difficulty. Some of the weaker stomachs had to settle accounts, but most stood the smell of the brine without a murmur. Passing the little island, of blue-clayey appearance, where once Fort Powell stood, in the neck of the bay, we began to see some of the obstructions which had impeded the advance of the Union fleet some months before. Lines of piles as far as the eye could reach extended across the bay. Touching for a few minutes at Fort Gaines, which had so opportunely surrendered in the preceding Fall, and passing the historic

Fort Morgan, which, terrible as we supposed it to be, looked like nothing more than a long, low sand-bank mounting one or two guns, we moved on up the bay, and entered the little harbor of Navy Cove, four miles above the extremity of Mobile Point.

Soon after landing, the advance-companies of the regiment marched over to the place assigned for our camp, on the gulf side of the point, and prepared for a stay of several days. Mobile Point is a strip of land, some four or five miles long, and about a quarter of a mile wide, extending from the mainland down between the gulf and the bay. Nearly the whole of it, at any rate, all the lower part, is a mere bank of sand, on one side washed to a series of low hillocks, by the endless surf of the gulf, and on the other, smoothed to a level beach, by the placid waters of the bay. Near Fort Morgan, at its lower extremity, were camped some regiments which had been there since the fort was captured. From the fort to the cove, extended a railroad, with a rolling-stock of a single locomotive, and a few platform-cars, sufficient to convey supplies from the landing.

Near the cove commenced a kind of swamp in the center of the point. This was filled with water, grass and alligators.

Around its edges were thickets of thorny bushes, strange weeds, and a kind of dwarf palmetto. A few straggling old houses stood near the landing, occupied by the families of pilots and oyster-men. North of these, and connecting with the bay, was a shallow pond, almost lined on the bottom with small mud-oysters. Beyond this, a rather heavy and swampy timber-land commenced, which seemed to have no limits but the horizon. The whole place seemed strange and wild, and in no wise like any country to which we had been accustomed. No description of it could convey a full and proper impression. Mobile Point was an episode in our military experience; and if at first, its novelty was pleasing to some, all at last agreed that it was an excellent place to get away from.

It was glorious fun for us, while the novelty lasted, to go out and bathe in the surf of the gulf in the hot forenoons; or to walk at night along the beach, where every step stirred up showers of phosphorescent sparkles, that looked as though the very sand were latent fire; or to wade for oysters in the shallow pond above the cove, and forget our baked heads and cut and bruised feet, in the tantalizing prospect of fried oysters for supper; or to gather a crowd on the edge of the little swamp, and endeavor to capture an alligator; or to watch the fairy-like sailing craft and war-like steamers, as they glided to and fro, so near us. All these were pleasant at first, but the novelty would not last forever. The discomforts, on the contrary, were present continually. There was endless heat above, and restless sand below,—sand, sand, sand in every thing. Mouths, noses, ears and even eyes were filled with it, and victuals were all seasoned with the everlasting and omnipresent nuisance. To partially balance this, was the strange but grateful fact, that we had only to dig holes a few feet deep in the sand, on the gulf side, to find plenty of the freshest and purest water.

On Monday afternoon, the remaining companies of the regiment arrived. On Wednesday, the 1st of March, Rev. P. P. Ingalls, agent of the Iowa State Orphans' Home, addressed us, and organized subscriptions for the Home; and next day addressed us again. Our regiment contributed four thousand and five hundred dollars. In a day or two after our landing at the cove, shelter-tents were issued to us, and were unanimously considered a very disagreeable novelty. We hated to huddle ourselves into little cloth kennels, hardly big enough for dogs. All despised them, and many savagely prophesied that before two days of marching, they would be all thrown away. Within a month, however, opinions changed; and the men who had so severely derided the dog-tents, were willing enough to carry them for the use they gave. Experience soon showed that they are decidedly better than no tent at all.

Company-drill was commenced on the 6th of March, more perhaps for the sake of exercise than for any other reason. On the 8th there was a brigade-inspection and review, under Major-General Osterhaus, which was a very tiresome affair, in the hot sun and sand. Far south as we were now, and advanced as was the season there, we were by no means beyond the reach of cold. Thursday night, the 9th of March, it was so cold that it was almost impossible to sleep, and we actually shivered, and suffered perhaps more than ever at night before. Saturday, the 11th, most of the gun-boats that were lying at and near the cove, cleared decks for action, and steamed off up the bay. During the day we heard from that direction the sound of heavy cannonading — that low, dull rumble of the gun-boat bolts, which afterward became so familiar.

The next Tuesday was a day of rain and discomfort. The most we could do was to stay in our little dog-tents and exist, in a sort of apathetic sullenness, like so many animals. The Chaplain, poor fellow! who was not so old a soldier as the rest of us, had pitched his dog-tent very carefully, but in a hollow of the sand; and the rain made almost a floating island of his habitation. The poor man got an old cracker-box and put it in the centre of his tent, piled himself on it, on his knees, wrapped in his blankets, and resigned himself to fate with a look of stoical endurance that would have shamed a martyr.

To make the situation more uncomfortable, some wretched jokers took turns through the day in going up to the front of his dog-tent, giving him one glance of mischievous commiseration, and then expressing their fellow-feeling by barking like dogs. Words would have been weak in comparison.

So, all the time the weather varied; rain and cold, sunshine and heat, each more intense by contrast. Perhaps we never had more little discomforts at one time, than crowded about us during our stay at Mobile Point; yet the memory of those days will always have a tinge of pleasantness, because every thing was so new and strange.

CHAPTER XVIII.

TO SPANISH FORT.

Short notice was given us of the march from Mobile Point. Our transportation was already cut down to the lowest notch; and there were standing orders, from head-quarters of the military division, that all the troops should hold themselves in readiness to march at a moment's notice. Having been assigned to the 3d Brigade, 3d Division, 13th Army Corps, our brigade-commander was Colonel Conrad Krez, of the 27th Wisconsin; division-commander, Brigadier-General Wm. P. Benton; and corps-commander, Major-General Gordon Granger. This organization was retained until we went to Texas.

Thursday afternoon, March 16th, the order came for us to move next morning, with three days' cooked rations in haversack. We had already on hand the rations that were to last us an additional day. Whatever may be the theoretical view of the case, it is practically certain that for a man to carry, in a sack slung over his shoulder, all he is to eat for four days, and this weight in addition to his knapsack, gun and rigging, is no laughing matter. That night, in the very nick of time, the long-looked-for mail arrived, with news from home about a month old. Next morning at 6:30, the march commenced. The day proved perfectly beautiful. Moving up the beach on the eastern side of the point, we soon entered the wood, left the gulf behind, and after a march of eight or ten miles, pitched camp in a very good place at about 2 P. M.

The next day's march was ten miles, through pine timber, over alternate marsh and sand. In the morning there was a jolly scene, when we waded across a small and shallow arm of the bay. The whole division formed in columns closed in mass; and at the word all proceeded to roll up their pants and prepare to wade. Wade it had to be, for there was no other way of crossing. It was a scene for a comic artist—those heavy columns of blue-coated infantry busily engaged in rolling up the legs of their pants until, like so many boys at play, they struck into the water, and with shouts and laughter waded easily across. Some where about noon, as we were marching through the interminable pine wood, the noise of merriment rose in front again. As we neared the place, the cause was seen. An old negro woman, apparantly half-crazed with joy at the sight of the Union army she and hundreds of the race, companions in suffering, had so long prayed for, was standing near the road as the column passed her, shouting, dancing, crying and laughing, almost hysterically, in the vain effort to express her overflowing feelings. "Glory, Hallelujah!" she shouted; "Glory Hallelujah! The Lord's done heard us! Glory! There's eight hundred of us praying for you at Mobile! Go on! Go on! Glory, Hallelujah!" And then the poor creature would dance, and shout and sing, cry and laugh, all at once, while the tears coursed down her worn and wrinkled cheeks as she beheld the army which to so great a portion of her race seemed the harbinger of jubilee, and almost as the coming of the Lord.

It was a pathetic yet ludicrous incident; and the smile mingled with the tear among us as we went marching on. It was no new thing to us, to be hailed by these bondmen as their

10

deliverers; yet if we some times stopped to think of it, there would come a strange question, how much we really deserved their gratitude? But thinking is the very least of a soldier's business; and so the incident and its impressions passed out of mind together, as the important trivialities of the march succeeded. Sunday night our camp was pitched in the midst of the endless forest of tall, straight, almost branchless pines. The ground was flat, smooth, clean and dry; and the camp would have been an excellent one if only wood and water had been near. It may seem odd that in a pine forest should be no wood to burn; but such is very nearly the actual fact. Green pine is abominable fire-wood. Pine knots were scattered around quite plentifully, and we used them for fuel; but they smoke the victuals so in cooking that the soldier will for that purpose, take any other wood in preference. Water was plenty, but not near camp; and what there was, was but a shallow pond where the rain-water had not yet had time to evaporate or become absorbed. A large camp of men and animals will use a great deal of water, and dirty up much more. Men must wash their faces and hands, at least, and to get water for coffee in the center of a little pool, all around whose edges men are washing hands and feet, is not calculated to make the coffee set well on a fastidious stomach.

The next day we lay in camp, waiting for our place in the train to come along, till about four in the afternoon; and then marched four or five miles. Across the road in one or two places lay the ugly carcasses of alligators, which some of the advance-party had killed and left there; and it was by no means nice to speculate upon the probability of having such an ungainly "insect" some night as a bed-fellow. To explain how alligators came in a dry-pine wood, it should be added that there were occasional ponds and swamps, and these were found near them. Being train-guard, our regiment was divided into two or three squads, and scattered among the train. As night drew on, of course the wagons stuck in the swamps worse than ever. To add to the beauties of the time, a heavy shower came up. It was late in the night when the right wing of the regiment, wet to the bone, chilled and tired, reached the place, where in the middle of a large turpentine-orchard, the camp had been pitched.

The term "turpentine-orchard" may for Northern readers need some explanation. Such an "orchard" in full vigor is a dense, unbroken forest of young pine trees, each of which at a certain age has been tapped by a large chip off one side. The turpentine slowly oozes from the wound, forms a thick coating over the abraded surface, and settles in the hollow at its bottom. Usually the trees are carefully tended, and the turpentine gathered at the proper time; but in this orchard the trees had been neglected, till there was now a thick mass of solidified turpentine on every one. There was warmth for us, and novelty withal; and soon the trees were blazing furiously. Each one would burn fifteen or twenty minutes before its supply of turpentine was exhausted. Whether the process was good for the tree or not, we really did not stop to inquire.

Wednesday was spent in sending back details, taking nearly all the troops by turns, to build corduroys for the last few miles of road, along which the train had "stuck" with remarkable uniformity. At one time, meanwhile, by some accident or carelessness, the forest had been set on fire not far from us; and now the huge volumes of smoke rose black and nearer. The bright, lurid flames played round the trunks of the trees, whose stores of turpentine increased the intensity of the conflagration, till it seemed as if the whole camp must perish, miserable but insignificant, in the glowing ruin of surrounding flames. But a certain feeling of terror was the only damage it caused us. Either because the fires of the preceding night had exhausted the combustibility of the trees near camp, or for some other reason, the fire did not come near enough to give us much real discomfort, beyond that vague but deep and "realizing" sense of what would be our own littleness and powerlessness if He who rules the elements had not restrained them.

The wagons having finally got out of the mud, we started on again next morning, moving nearly all the way through the unvarying pine wood, but noting with a real feeling of welcome and joy, the appearance of trees and bushes of a more familiar leaf and living green, as we neared Fish River. This deep and narrow stream we crossed at about half-past two P. M., of the 23d, on a wooden pontoon-bridge which had been laid by men sent around on boats before us. By order from General Benton, every band in our division struck up "Out of the Wilderness" as its regiment crossed the bridge. Moving on up to the high grounds a mile or so from the river, we were marched and counter-marched in various places, and stopped and formed in camp-arrangement here and there, to see how the brigade would fit the ground; and finally settled down to camp.

General A. J. Smith's command, the 16th Army Corps, had arrived here before us. As it was expected we would take some little rest before the whole column moved on farther, the camp was, therefore, laid out with great care and regularity, wells dug, sinks provided, and arrangements made as if we might remain a month. We were now part of the largest army with which we had ever been, and therefore felt "invincible against any force the enemy might send against us." Soon after we had camped, another mail was distributed, strengthening and cheering us with the thought that we were "though absent, not forgotten."

Saturday, the 25th, the column commenced moving in the morning; and by half-past three in the afternoon, it had stretched out so that we took our place in the line of march. We made but about six or eight miles that evening, and then camped so far a head of the wagons, that they did not come up that night. The consequence was, that many a poor officer, whose blankets and provisions were in the train, had to lie down supperless, on the bare and chilling ground, and take what little sleep he could, by the warmth only of the half-tended pine-knot fires. Sunday brought no rest. Rising early, we marched on as usual; and at night camped within two miles of the "Spanish Fort" which was expected to hinder further progress. A change of employment for us, was now to come.

CHAPTER XIX.

THE SIEGE.

Sun-rise of Monday, the 27th of March, saw us in arms, and making ready to move forward. The command was finally formed in column by battalion, properly placed and directed, and at 9:30 the advance commenced. There were frequent stops, mysterious runnings to and fro of officers and orderlies, changes of position by artillery and skirmishers, and all the usual indications of premeditated battle. At 10:20, occasional artillery-firing began, and at a quarter after 11 the first rattle of musketry was heard on our left. The siege had commenced.

Some where within a mile of the rebel fort, our regiment was halted, and lay till nearly dark. Meanwhile a rain came on. Having nothing else to do, we huddled under the trees for shelter, while occasionally some one would go to the front to see what was going on. Early in the evening we were moved forward to our position in the main line of attack which was thrown almost entirely around the land-side of the rebel works, and rested at either extremity upon the bay. Our regiment was the extreme right of the 13th corps; and the 16th corps extended its left around to join us. In the first day of the siege there was much reckless and unpardonable risking of life. Some regiments, for no possible reason but the drunken bravado of general officers, were for hours held in the most exposed positions, in close formation, without shelter of any kind. It was fortunate for the 33d that we were not so ordered. The field-pieces in our main line of attack kept up an occasional firing till some time after dark, but the rebels did not reply very much. This seemed like weakness then; but we afterward learned that they had their guns double-shotted with grape and canister all the time, in readiness for the charge they expected us to make, and from which few of us could have ever returned.

Night at last brought quiet. At day-light next morning, a single bugle sounded reveille; and soon the "ball opened" again. Heavy details were kept on the skirmish-line, and relieved in the day-time. This was all wrong. Several men were wounded while being thus relieved; and soon the details refused to be relieved in the day-time, preferring to remain in their shallow lines, and holes of partial safety, rather than to risk the full exposure of their persons so near the rebel works, for the mere sake of coming back to camp. The time of relieving was therefore changed, and a company or two at a time sent out. The number of casualties was from this time much smaller.

Corporal Haydock, of Company E, describes one or two incidents so vividly as to give a very good picture of the skirmish-line, which was the main scene of action during the siege. The following are very nearly his own words:

"On the night of the 29th of March the enemy charged us and attempted to capture our advanced line. Our company was sent before day-light on the morning of the 29th, to relieve Company K on that portion of the skirmish-line directly opposite our regiment. We left camp about three o'clock in the morning, with a day's rations and one hundred rounds of cartridges. Arriving in the vicinity of the rebel fort, we had to march very stealthily to prevent the enemy from hearing and slaughtering us before we reached our ditch. The road was a miserable one to advance over, being covered with fallen trees, whose tops pointed mostly outward. Every now and then a minnie ball would whiz through the air close to our heads, making us dodge, and think it was aimed for no one especially. Once in a while we would come to a deep and narrow pit, containing two or three "bummers" who had let their courage ooze out at their fingers-end before they reached the front ditch. These fellows would lie in their holes all day, and fire at the enemy over the heads of the men in advanced line, making them wonder if they were not in more danger from friends than foes.

Deploying our line, we advanced with a considerable low whistling and other signaling, to the works which had been thrown up the night before by Company K, close to the enemy's line. I was considerably amused at the Dutch (27th Wisconsin) who were on our left. When I came up, I came on them. By that time, the enemy were firing very briskly. I asked one of the Dutchmen where our company was. "Get town here, G— tam you!" was all the response I could get. After blundering and stumbling around for some time, I got to our ditch. The Dutch were now relieved; but one of them was left in the ditch asleep. One of our boys shook him, and asked him if he did not belong to the regiment that was relieved. He roused himself up, and replied that he did. We told him to go on to camp, and he started to go; but the flash from the enemy's guns, accompanied by a warning from some of us to "keep low," so frightened the poor boy that he commenced describing a circle, and performing various other antic feats, which reminded me very much of a pig with the "blind staggers." "Here, this way, this way," said some one, pointing with his finger. "Vich vay, vich vay?" replied the poor frightened boy, as he climbed over our works and was on the point of running over toward the rebel fort. Some one caught him by the heels and dragged him back into our ditch; and after a deal of crawling and creeping, hither and thither, he started off in the right direction, and we saw him no more.

By this time it was growing light; and we found ourselves in front of the rebel fort, so that we could pour our fire directly into their embrasures. Before it grew too light, we busied ourselves in improving our ditch, by digging it deeper and throwing the dirt over in front for protection. Through the day we watched the enemy's embrasures so closely that they could not use their guns with any effect. At one embrasure they ran out a huge, grim monster of a siege-gun, but we kept up such a peppering that they were glad to withdraw it without firing. About this time the large rebel fort opened upon our skirmish-line. We would closely watch the huge pile of yellow dirt seen dimly in the distance; and presently we would see a dense volume of smoke rising, and "down" would be our warning. Down we would fall, to the bottom of the ditch. In a few seconds we would hear a loud explosion, and looking in its direction would see the smoke curling up in fantastic wreaths from where the shell had burst.

We were directly between the rebel fort and one of our own batteries, which opened during the day, so that our own shots passed directly over our heads. One struck very near us, and and bounded over toward the enemy. Another exploded close to our ditch. By this time we began to fear our friends. In the afternoon, the enemy appeared very anxious to drive us from our advanced position, and accordingly planted a small mortar so as to bear on us, and fired it at regular intervals. Whenever we heard the report we would watch closely, and could see the huge, round missile slowly ascending, describing a curve like a large foot-ball, and then it would come to the ground with a terrible explosion. In the afternoon I became so fatigued that I went to sleep, with the shells bursting all around me, and the minnie balls whizzing above. I had never before imagined that one could sleep in such circumstances.

The rebels were in the habit of passing before a certain embrasure. J. E. Young, of our company, had his rifle leveled at the place with his finger on the trigger, when a "yellow-coat" passed the opening. He pulled, and down went the Johnny. Another one came along and picked him up. That night, half of us wrapped ourselves in our gum blankets and lay down to sleep; but the rain pelted us so heavily we could not sleep much. At mid-night my relief came on. I sat down in the ditch, with my blanket wrapped around me, thinking how comfortable it would be to be some where else, when suddenly I heard a sharp, heavy rattling of musketry on our left, accompanied by loud cheering. At the same time our vedette gave the warning "The enemy is advancing upon us." Three times he gave the warning, without ever flinching or giving back, although the rebels were close upon him; and then he climbed up into the ditch.

I awakened the boys as quickly as possible; and Sergeant Redpath gave the order "Fix your bayonets, men; and when they come up, punch them back." This order, in his cool, deliberate tone, served to re-assure the men; and in less than a minute every man was loading and firing rapidly. "Buzz, buzz," went the bullets over our heads; but a perfect stream of fire from our ditch kept the enemy at bay. The ditch was too deep for some of us to fire with ease, so we climbed out and gave it to them. Our boys did bravely. We had no chance for retreat, so every man determined to measure bayonets if it were necessary. The enemy had determined to capture our skirmish-line that night, as we had crawled too close for their gunners to work their guns. But our boys convinced them that night that Mobile was a doomed city."

The duty of the main lines of infantry, drawn around the rebel works, was simply to protect themselves, and furnish the tremendous details. Not only the regiments themselves had to be protected by breast-works, but every head-quarters, from brigade on up, must have a heavy line of earth-works in front of it. The artillery-fire of the rebels was not slacked after the first day; and there was great need of protection. Shot and shell occasionally came altogether too close to be convenient. The country immediately around Spanish Fort seemed to have been specially formed for us to lay the siege. Deep gullies, separated of course by ridges or knolls of earth, formed a rough likeness to concentric circles which, connected by the heavy breast-works of logs and dirt, constructed in profusion in an almost incredibly short time, constituted our parallel lines of approach and defense. To aid the fitness of the place, an excellent and copious brook ran at a convenient distance, and good springs gushed from the little hills. Evidently nature had intended Spanish Fort to be besieged.

There was now a certain monotony about the days. Very heavy details were sent out to work on the fortifications; and as their work drew near a close, or became of less importance, they would be relieved by smaller details, or discontinued. One night Lieutenant-Colonel Lofland had been out with a detail of three hundred men; and in the morning a corporal came out with his squad and relieved him. Perhaps that is the only instance where, in due military order, a field officer was relieved by a corporal. The companies out on the skirmish-line, two at a time from each regiment, had occupation enough, having approached so near the opposing line that frequent conversations took place between them and the rebels. A miniature commerce in coffee and tobacco was at least much talked of, if not carried into actual effect; for as there were no sutlers' shops allowed with this expedition, tobacco had now become almost as scarce with us, as coffee among the rebels. Stories were told of a lieutenant leading his men by mistake into the enemy's skirmish-line, and of his learning his error and moving back to his own proper base, with an ease that only the darkness of the night and the nearness of the contestants to each other could account for.

The body of the regiment, as well as of the other parts of the main line, had merely to construct the necessary protections—a work which proved no trifle. The din of reveille dwindled down to a bugle in the early morning; and no sound of bugle or drum was allowed during the day; yet brass bands at the different general head-quarters would make the wood ring with their practice for hours together. We were now for the first time in a regular siege. There was no time in the day when one could feel at all certain that some rebel bullet or shell might not come singing or whistling along especially for him; but it must not be inferred that we considered this uncertainty always as a very serious matter. There were times, indeed, when no one would travel around more than he had good cause for; but much of the time there were men scattered along the brook, washing, or traveling between the line of attack, and the hospitals and trains, which kept themselves at a safe distance in the rear.

Occasionally there were some narrow escapes. One of these was particularly noticeable. In that part of the line which

Company D occupied, there was the stump of a tree, which had been cut down for the breast-works. One day a number of men were standing around it, chatting, when a shell came over, and cut in two a musket sticking in the ground near by, struck the stump, and passed on without hitting any person. Those who were there, said that it would seem impossible for any thing to hit the stump, without going through some one of the men, who were gathered so close around it.

Wednesday night, the 29th, the rebels made a bold sortie, and penetrated almost to the main line of our works. There was confusion in camp for a few minutes; but the affair did not last long. The rebels went back more hastily than they came, and gained nothing by their daring. Reports and rumors were now thicker than ever. The rebels at Mobile were doing this, and were going to do that. They were going to surrender, to hold out to the last, to charge on us, and to retreat. In fact, there was nothing they were not going to do, (and we too), except what was really done. On the morning of the 31st, the regiment to the right of us, having moved away, our regiment took a "side step to the right," and occupied their place. They had not only built a heavy breast-work in front of their position, but had constructed bomb-proofs of logs and dirt, partially dug in the ground, enough to shelter themselves entirely. For some cause or other, we had not yet made any protection for ourselves, except the earth-work in front, as ordered, although, nearly or quite all the other troops in the line, had done a great deal of such work; but now upon moving into bomb-proofs already made, we went at work and enlarged and strengthened them. The whole ground was dug in holes, and looked like an oblong of gigantic burrowers. This was by no means useless labor. The firing was of course irregular, and some times almost entirely ceased; but there were spells, as always just before sun-set, when the artillery on both sides would open briskly, and then, when the rebel shot and shell began to whistle closer over us, the bomb-proofs were welcome and crowded; and it was not cowardice but common-sense, which demanded the protection.

About sun-down of the 31st there was a decidedly lively time for a few minutes. The cannonading on both sides was heavier than it had been before; and piles of brush lying between the opposing lines were set on fire, either by accident or intentionally, and lit up the scene to almost grandeur. Though the siege had now lasted but four or five days, we felt already well used to it. The regular booming of the half-hour guns was an accustomed sound; and the lively contest of artillery just before sun-down was looked for as a thing of course. Soldiers soon learn to adapt themselves to circumstances. The routine of camp was readily adjusted to the place, and followed with as cheerful carelessness as ever. Laughing and joking abounded.

For several days there had been talk of an issue of tobacco by the quarter-master. It seemed almost too good to be true; but on the 3d of April the tobacco came, almost as welcome as pay-day or a mail. On Wednesday morning, the 5th of the month, the 7th Minnesota came back to their old position, and we had to vacate. A new place was assigned us, about a mile further to the left but in the same main line. It had been occupied by some other regiment, and was almost honey-combed with bomb-proof works, which did not seem to be very effective; and our first business therefore, was to enlarge and improve them, until at last we made them so snug, that many of us would have almost been willing to stay there for the rest of our term of service.

The firing grew all the time heavier. On the evening of the 8th, the gun-boats, which had been taking part but occasionally in the contest, began launching their tremendous bolts in solid earnest. As darkness came on, the scene approached the sublime. The bay was entirely hidden from us by the wooded hills, but the shells from the gun-boats could be distinctly seen as with majestic slowness they described their brilliant arcs, and fell point-blank in the rebel fort almost at the instant of explosion. The gunners seemed to have got the range perfectly. On land, too, the siege-guns which had been so long in coming up, were now in position; and for about an hour on the evening of the 8th there was such a cannonading as we had never heard before. The whole artillery force of our army and gun-boats opened in one terrible storm of fire, so concentrated on the rebel fort that it seemed almost impossible for it to endure a repetition.

That evening we noticed a little circumstance, which seemed odd to us then, and which in earlier days might have hastened exertions on to victory, or been accepted as an omen of defeat. The evening was clear, and the moon shone bright in the southern sky. Some where about 8 o'clock, we saw three very small halos, or circles, of various colors, like the rain-bow, around the moon. The effect was weird and beautiful. Ordinary "rings around the moon" are common enough; but three small rings, brightly and variously colored, in the midst of a cloudless sky, were to us as novel as they were beautiful. There were some who thought the sight portended some thing; and perhaps it did.

That afternoon and evening there was much heavier cannonading some distance up the bay, than we had heard before. General Steele with his negroes was evidently pounding away at Blakely; but there seemed to be nothing new in store for us, and we went to sleep as usual. About mid-night a shout arose. Our forces, pressing closer on the rebel lines, had found the fort just evacuated; and with joy and tumult they rushed in and took possession. The thirteen days of siege at last were ended. We were vexed that the rebels had succeeded in retreating; but to have driven them from their strong-hold was cause enough for joy. Many of our regiment were so eager and excited, that they could not wait till morning, but tumbled out of bed, and went up to see the fort by moon-light.

Sunday morning, the 9th, was rainy and disagreeable. Reveille was sounded on the drums for the first time since the commencement of the siege. Orders soon came for us to be ready to move immediately; but not all of us could restrain the curiosity to see what we had been so long fighting about, and so we had to go up and see the fort. A strange sensation came over us as we climbed, unhindered, over the breast-works and walls, from which a few hours before we would have been swept off with a storm of fire had we attempted to scale them. We were glad enough no "charge" had been ordered; glad, indeed that our position had been on the out-side and not inside the fort, the center of such a rain of iron and lead, it showed the marks of conflict every where. There was hardly a square yard of ground in or near the fort which was not torn by shot or shell. Along tho top of the inner wall, logs a foot or so in diameter were laid, as protection for the heads of the sharp-shooters stationed behind them; and one of these logs, on the side opposite that part of the line last held by our regiment, was so scarred that not a finger could have been laid on it without covering the mark of a bullet.

The fort — or rather, Battery Huger, as the name of the main work seemed to be — must have been a terribly hot and uncomfortable place during the bombardment. Looking at the traces of ruin and devastation around, one would hardly think it possible that human beings could have lived there and worked the guns, under such a storm of death as beat upon them; and indeed we remember that during the last two days the rebel fire had gently slackened, and finally dwindled to nothing. But the fort evidently had been well supplied with arms and ammunition. Some of the cannon had within the month been cast at the Selma Arsenal. The largest gun, a splendid one-hundred-and-twenty-pound Brook's rifled, had been dismounted by a shot from one of our batteries or gun-boats. The other ordnance was numerous enough, but very various in construction and caliber, though none of them were heavy.

All around the fort, at a suitable distance from the outer walls, the ground was planted with torpedoes set in a double line, such as would be described by the corners of a common rail-fence made with rails a foot or two shorter than usual. The effect of thus planting them, was that no column of men, even so small as four abreast, could have passed over the line without hitting the torpedoes. This same diabolical plan of defense we afterward found in use at Blakely—diabolical, because it was as likely to work destruction after the contest was over, as while it lasted, or even more so; as likely to kill the victor as the enemy. A description of the torpedo may not be useless.

A heavy shell of cast-iron, about the average size of a twenty-four-pound round shot, is perforated with two holes. One of these serves simply to admit or draw out the powder, and is usually secured by a screw cap. Through the other hole runs down a compound substance that communicates the fire to the powder that fills the shell. At the upper part of the substance is a material which will ignite under a sudden pressure of about four pounds. Over this, when the torpedo is in the arsenal, is screwed a thick and solid safety-cap; but for actual use, this heavy cap is taken off, and an inner one exposed, consisting of copper so thin that a pressure of four pounds will force it down suddenly upon the explosive compound beneath. The torpedo so prepared, is set in the ground just enough to let the thin cap appear above the surface. Any ordinary foot-step will now cause the explosion, which will in all probability shatter to fragments every thing near it.

The torpedo was an unaccustomed weapon of warfare to us; and it was perhaps for this reason that many, if not most of us, feared them more than bullet or shell. Men, who would have hardly been careful enough of themselves against the missiles of the battle, were very dubious as to torpedoes, and would examine the ground minutely for the little sticks which served to mark the place where a torpedo was buried. At Spanish Fort, as afterward at Blakely, several men were killed by the explosion of torpedoes, after the grounds came into our possession. At Blakely, after the rebel works were captured, squads of the rebel prisoners were set at work, taking up the torpedoes which encircled their lines; but it is probable that many of them were overlooked. Likely enough, the farmer who shall yet plow over the land, where the outer lines of Spanish Fort and Blakely extended, may suddenly strike the cap of one of these terrible shells, and be blown to pieces. Thus the weapon the father prepared, may turn against the son.

For protection from the tremendous fire of our artillery, the rebels in the fort had dug holes and winding ways in the ground, inside the works. It was said that after its evacuation, a number of sick and wounded were found in these holes, and that two or three days afterward, a rebel officer of rather high rank, was found concealed at the extremity of one of the covered ways. But we could not stop to explore much. Another regiment was detailed as guards at the fort, and we were of the number ordered forward.

CHAPTER XX.

HITHER AND THITHER.

Breaking camp on the morning of the 9th, without a thought of its being Sunday, we formed line a little way out in the wood, and drew rations while halting for a few moments. There seemed some thing almost ludicrous in the idea of issuing those two barrels of sour kraut, with the other rations, to men all in line and ready for the march, and whose only means of carrying food was in their haversacks; and in fact the kraut disappeared so fast in other ways that it was not issued. Military discipline and routine are some times so absurdly impossible, that on some occasions harm results from the lack of a reasonable approach to them.

The march of Sunday was of only ten miles' length, but was very tiresome. On the way, the knowledge spread that we were being pushed forward to Blakely to take part in a charge on the rebel works there. Some time before we reached the place, however, the news met us that the charge had been made, and the victory won. We were badly behindhand, but it was no fault of ours. The charge had been made before the expected time — without orders, we were told — and won by the most recklessly desperate fighting. Had it not been for a sort of Western independence and individuality of action among the troops composing General Steele's command—negroes though many if not most of them were—we should have had part in this last important action of the war.

Next day, the 11th of April, lying in camp about a mile from the rebel works, we had time to rest and look around. A heavy mail, arriving the night before, had given us the latest news from home, and was forthwith answered by one almost as heavy. Many of us spent the forenoon in looking at the prisoners taken, and examining the rebel works. One squad of prisoners, comprising part of an Alabama regiment, was camped near us, in charge of a detail of negroes. We could not but observe that these Alabamians were a very different class of men from those to whom we had been accustomed in Arkansas. More nearly in uniform, with their strong and active physique and hearty bearing, they looked more like "foemen worthy of our steel." Between them and the negroes, however, there seemed to be some old grudge to settle. No display of feeling against the prisoners was allowed to be manifested: there was no sign of "crowing" over a fallen foe, no taunting or insult allowed or attempted; but we could often hear expressions of the deepest hate and vindictiveness from dusky lips when away from the line of guards. Who shall know how many and deep tragedies lay there concealed; what wrongs but partially redressed; what burning sense of injustice and shame that called so grimly for the captive masters' blood!

The rebel works at Blakely were extensive, as indeed the rebel works in Alabama always were—always such as would require a force from two to ten times as great as they could ever have, to properly man them. Whose the fault may have been, we could not tell, but its existence was always noticed. Little as we might understand of the theoretical art of war, we had for ourselves fully learned that earth-works, to be effectively available, must not be too extensive for the force likely to defend them. At Pine Bluff, Arkansas, General Clayton had resisted repeated attacks from a force greatly out-numbering his own command; and we could plainly see that his success was partially due to the great concentration of his lines of defense.

The town of Blakely, so far as we could discover, existed almost solely in name. We were told that there had once been a number of fine houses there, and that the town was a well-known watering-place for the beauty and fashion of Mobile. No semblance of such prestige now remained. At the usual landing-place on the bank of the Tensas river, a large crane had apparently been just scared out of the job of mounting a couple of heavy cannon which lay near it, just arrived from the Selma Arsenal. One small frame-building, formerly a grocery, now stood dirty and empty by the street. Several wall-tents, made of the coarse but strong cotton cloth which plainly showed its Southern manufacture, were used as hospitals, and filled with rebel sick and wounded. And a large shed, which had been used as the arsenal, was well stored with torpedoes, shell, shot and other weapons, with the remains of such quarter-master's and ordnance papers as the absconding officials had not taken away. Many of these scraps of paper, of evidently Southern manufacture, were gathered to be sent North; but their interest is now only that which can attach to the millions of similar relics which may be found in the thousands of Northern homes.

The left of the rebel line of defense rested on the deep and narrow Tensas river, of which this bank was a bluff some twenty feet in hight, and the opposite was a low, swampy flat; and its continuation was a series of earth-work, aggregated at every salient point into batteries of varying strength and size, interspersed with palisades and isolated pieces of artillery, and additionally strengthened by the most impregnable abattis we had ever seen, piled high in double, triple, and some times quadruple rows. How men could charge over such lines of defense, we, ourselves not wholly ignorant of warfare, could not imagine; but probably if we had been in the fight we should have known as well as any, and done our share. A negro soldier, who was in the terrible charge, understood the matter in its practical application. As he stood near the works, examining the ground over which his regiment had gone into the rebel lines, the lines of sharp-pointed brush and limbs of trees rose piled up higher than his head. He was a powerful fellow, of the purest African blood, and with all the African fire and fervor. When asked how on earth the men could ever have charged over that most formidable abattis, his eyes glistened, and his quick tongue found the ready though uncouth answer: "Golly, mass'r! Nebber knowed dat ar brush-pile was dar!"

Artillery, ammunitions, rations and all the material of war, seemed to have been abundant among the rebels; and their capture in such quantities, at an early period of the war, would have been considered worthy of conspicuous mention. Now, it was over-shadowed, even among ourselves, by the news of the capture of Richmond. At last, after all the lingering years of uncertainty and effort, Richmond was indeed ours! Often before, in our varied service, we had cheered over reports of its capture; but now, when the news was joyful, and almost undoubted truth, there rose not a cheer. With deep, but quiet thankfulness and joy, we felt that the "backbone of the rebellion" was now indeed broken, and peace must be near. We could endure till the end should come.

There were reports many, and hopes many. Much speculation was hazarded as to the surrender of Mobile. Some man over in the rebel works, early in the morning, looking across the flats and bay, to where the city of Mobile was dimly visible, had discovered some thing there, which seemed to him to be a white flag waving. He called to some one else, and the look was doubled, with the same result. All day long there was a group collected on the spot, continuing the observation; and all arrived at the same belief, though to all it seemed almost impossible, that they could see a white flag floating over Mobile.

Receiving orders on Monday, to be ready to march at a moment's warning, we lay in camp till Tuesday evening, the 11th; and by that time there came news that Mobile was evacuated. The report that reached us, was to the effect that our division-commander had received the news, and, intoxicated with joy, or some thing else, had sworn that his division should be the first to enter Mobile. Some thing of the kind seemed to be in the wind; for at about dark on Tuesday evening, we broke camp again, and turned to retrace our steps toward Spanish Fort. The night was beautifully moon-lit; the report of the evacuation was more than half-credited; and we started out in high spirits, singing and laughing as we marched along. But the tramp proved exceedingly tiresome, before it ended.

Colonel Krez, of the 27th Wisconsin, then commanding our brigade, had managed to acquire the reputation of never getting on the right road. Coming up to Colonel Mackey, at Spanish Fort, one day, he had complained of the bad conduct of some of our boys. "Dey says me Chris," he urges; "dey calls me lose de vay. As I catch 'em, I punish 'em bad."

In our ignorance of the occult principles of "military necessity," after the head-quarter's interpretation, we could not feel at all delighted, at being on different occasions put under the command of bloated beer-casks, whose only antecedents were, that they used to keep a saloon. On this mid-night march, when all were tired to the last extreme of unmurmuring endurance, of course the worthy brigade-commander must lose the road. Against the advice of his staff-officers and others, and in default of precautions which ordinary common sense would have provided, he led us off on a wrong track, and had to waste perhaps an hour of marching, before we were finally set right again. The curses of the tired soldiers were loud and deep.

At about two in the morning we reached the bay at Stark's landing, two or three miles south of Spanish Fort. Here we were to take steamers to cross the bay; but were compelled to lie around on the sand, as best we might, and wait for day-light. As early as practicable on the morning of Wednesday, the 12th, we embarked on the fine steamer *General Banks*, used then as the head-quarters of General Granger, whose corps only was moving; and so commenced the crossing for the occupation of Mobile. The morning was foggy; but soon the sun shone out merrily upon the rippling waters, and lit up a scene of military splendor such as we had never beheld. Transports and gun-boats, in single or double lines, with signal-flags rising and falling, and colors proudly flying from the mast-head, moved slowly but majestically across the bay. One or two of the gun-boats were provided with machines for raising the torpedoes with which it was feared the course was strewn; but no trouble occurred. As we neared the western shore there was a greatly-increased display of signal-flags. One gun-boat advanced some distance ahead of the fleet, and threw a single shell as challenge to the shore; but no answer came. Again the signal-flags waved bravely. The gun-boat on which were the head-quarters of the fleet now moved nearer to the *General Banks*, and the portly and bedizened form of Admiral Thatcher appeared majestic on her deck. Turning dignifiedly toward our boat, with a slow and rotund pomposity of manner that words could not convey, he called out "I-propose-to-shell-the-shore." "By ——, you'll shell a flag of truce if you do," profanely answered General Granger. The ludicrousness of the situation became apparent when on looking shoreward we saw that all this tremendous array of "fleets, armies and artillery" was thus to be brought to bear against a solitary negro, whose feeble hand waved a white kerchief tremblingly.

It had been the intention to take our regiment to Mobile by boat, but upon further consideration it was not deemed wise to hazard so many lives against the torpedoes which were known to obstruct the channel. The General therefore went on in the boat, and we disembarked over the rotten and broken old wharf at Codfish landing. A delay of an hour or two ensued, and then we fell in with the column, and marched on toward the city, over the "shell road" of which we had heard so much, and of which too much could not be said in praise. Hard as a rock and smooth as a floor, it wound for five miles along the edge of the bay, shaded by beautiful trees and adorned by the neat though humble residences of the Creole population. It was such a delightful change from the rough places where we had usually been, that it must ever hold a place among our bright memories of pleasant scenes.

Still more and better news from the Potomac, drifted through the higher channels of official information, now came down to us. Not only was Richmond taken, but Lee's army was captured, and Petersburg ours. We could believe it now —and nothing seemed too good to believe. The war must be now virtually ended; and we felt sure of soon seeing home. Such was our feeling as we went into camp that night, on a nice, green field, near a part of the main defenses of Mobile, designated as battery K. Among all the extensive earthworks with which we were now environed, this was the most elaborate and completely finished we had ever seen; and citizens near there said it was the pride of the rebel engineers. Artillery abounded along all the works; and had the Johnnies made a stand they could have given us serious trouble. If they had been Yankees, or at any rate, if they had been Western men, they would never have bloodlessly yielded all those elaborate lines of defense simply because the enemy had captured the works across the bay. Near this part of the line had been a rebel camp, evidently hastily abandoned. Numerous relics were obtained here; and many were the cedar canteens which our boys afterward carried as mementoes of Mobile.

Next morning there were strict orders to the effect that no man or officer should leave camp to go to town. The orders were much more strict than was the obedience to them. Men had not fought and marched and waited all those weary days before Mobile, to now quietly be deprived of perhaps their only chance to see the city. That night there were many men for extra duty, brought to it by unauthorized absence from camp when the roll was called in the morning. A little before noon we were called into line; and our division marched on through the city with colors flying, drum-corps doing their noisy best, and as much display as the ragged and dirty condition of the uniforms would allow. Every body, except the white folks, turned out to see us. Little delay was allowed. The rebels had retreated up the Mobile and Ohio railroad; and forthwith up the railroad we started after them. At the little town called Whistler, some five miles out from Mobile, were located the manufacturing- and engine-shops of the road; and word had been received that the rear-guard of the rebels had just been committing depredations there.

Marching on a railroad is no pleasant way of traveling. It does very well for a while; but one soon gets tired of straddling from tie to tie, especially if he wears a knapsack. Reaching Whistler at last, we piled all our baggage, except fighting-gear, on the ground, and prepared for a skirmish. Our regiment went forward some distance on the double-quick, but could not come in soon enough. Other regiments, reaching town in advance of us, had done the business. The enemy was only a squad of some two hundred rebel cavalry, as we afterward learned, who had remained behind the main body of the army for the sake of plunder. Had their number been known at the time, there would have seemed some thing ridiculous in rushing to attack them with a whole division of infantry; but they made quite a resistance, as it was, and in the skirmish three of our force and sixteen rebels were killed.

This was the last preparation for battle that we ever saw; and our part of it ended in standing near the railroad for a few hours, and then, toward dark, going into camp, in the wood, in a nice place near town. Next morning, of course, the camp had to be moved again; and then we fixed ourselves up as if to stay for some time, which we really more than half expected. We could not see that there was any further fighting to be done; and the best probabilities seemed to be, that we should remain there in camp, till ordered home for muster-out. But in military matters, as in life generally, the most unexpected thing, is the very one that is sure to happen. The boys were always ready enough to form acquaintances among the ladies of any place, where we might happen to stop; and at Whistler, perhaps on account of our prospective stay there, a peculiarly auspicious commencement for society was made. It seemed too bad to see all these dreams of rest and comfort shattered; but we must be of those to whom "there is no peace."

CHAPTER XXI.

UP THE TOM B.

Wednesday, April 19th, reveille came at 3:30 in the morning; and in two hours we were on the march again. Though only seven or eight miles were accomplished that day, and camp was reached before two o'clock; it was a very hard march, on account of the intense heat, and the length of time we went without stopping. There should be short halts, of perhaps five minutes' duration, made regularly every half-hour, by a column of infantry, on the march; and unless some such precaution is carefully observed, especially in the heat of a Southern climate, there will result much misery, which might be avoided.

There is some thing strange and peculiar in going into camp in the wood at night, as we did on the 20th. When the regiment is near the rear of the column, and all the others get into camp and settled, before we come up, and the gloomy Southern forests are made all the more gloomy and picturesque, by the blazing camp-fires piercing the darkness, every tree and bush, and hollow in the ground, takes a new aspect as imagination tries to picture the general appearance of the place. Here, you fancy, must be a deep ravine; and off at the left there must be a river—the trees appearing to open, so that you want to walk down to the water's edge to see farther. So one always tries to form some general idea of the ground of camp; but when the morning comes, lo! all is changed. What you thought was the ravine, proves to have been but a couple of logs; the supposed river is only the edge of a prairie, or of a cleared spot in the wood; and the whole scenery, which last night you fancied must be so novel, and pleasant, is now by day-light, as common and prosaic, as the increasing light of age shows most of our youthful illusions to be.

"Reveille at 3 o'clock," was the order again on Friday morning; and hardly had the drums and fifes ceased their rattle and squeak, when the rain began to patter too. Getting up in the morning, and making fires, and cooking coffee and hard-tack, in the midst of a soaking rain, is very easy to write about, but not the most cheering and comfortable of realities. It has a tendency to make soldiers either very grum, or very jolly; and generally we chose the latter, which proved to be the better way.

Early in the forenoon we passed through the grounds of the United States Arsenal at Mt. Vernon, which was unanimously pronounced to be among the loveliest spots our ennuied eyes had seen. The place appeared now to be deserted, but not much injured. If we had been ordered to stop and garrison the arsenal, we would have obeyed with even more cheerfulness than the army regulations require. But we were not the fortunate ones. The word soon passed round that the 29th Iowa was to remain, and that we were to go on a few miles further, and build a fort.

How reports and conjectures start in the army, we used always to wonder, and shall probably find out when it is discovered "who struck Billy Patterson." Frequently the rumors are far enough from the actual truth; but generally they have some little foundation, though the fact at the bottom is usually so distorted by the accretion of opinions and surmises, that the man who first told the story would never recognize it after the fourth expedition. Some thing of the same kind may have been observed in civil life; but so numerous and definite and positive are the rumors of a camp, or an army, that it became a standing joke to tell that the commanding General was coming down to our quarters, some evening to hear the news and learn what was going to be done.

From the arsenal to our camp that night, the march was not long, but it was a hard one. The rain that had been resting for a while, commenced again with renewed vigor, and soon drenched every thing. Every gully was a creek, and every creek a river. The very road itself, for perhaps a mile or two at a time, on the more level places, was covered with water, through which the splashing column waded drippingly. At half-past 11 our camp was reached, in a pine swamp, near the Tombigbee river. Much difficulty was experienced by our accomplished brigade-commander, in finding the worst possible place for us, and even more than the usual marching and counter-marching in consequence ensued; but finally the ground was chosen so that the whole brigade might rest in line. Military discipline, as interpreted by martinets, may require that in a mere bivouac for a night or two, not less than in regular Winter-quarters, the whole force must be disposed in strict line and order, whatever else may be the result; but Common Sense, if it had ever had the pleasure of commanding a body of soldiers, would, on all such occasions as this, have consented to much irregularity of line for the sake of the comfort the men would gain by having the best ground for camp.

On Sunday, April 23d, the terrible news reached us of the assassination of the President. The blow was so sudden and so strange that we could hardly realize it; but there was left no room for doubt. The feeling with which the terrible event was met in the North will never be forgotten; and to this feeling in all its force we added a certain wrath and vengefulness. We felt as they may feel who see their homes destroyed by Indians. Had we been allowed the privilege of meeting twice our number of rebels then, there would have been no prisoners taken. But we had seen our last enemy in arms; and this rage gradually died away, leaving only that deep grief which the whole loyal nation felt, and must forever feel, over the mighty fallen. Never was man so loved as Abraham Lincoln.

Two days of rest gave us an opportunity of cleaning the mud off our clothes, and part of the rust from our guns. Tuesday morning, the 25th, the left wing of the regiment was sent up the river about ten miles, to McIntosh's Bluff, on the gunboat *Octorora*; and the remainder of the regiment went up on the *Jennie Rogers* in the afternoon. McIntosh's Bluff, dignified by the title of navy-yard, contained one old dwelling-house, three or four new and unpainted frame buildings, a saw-mill and a black-smith's shop. At a little distance from the river there were also several log buildings, which had been used as quarters by the mechanic's who worked at the yard. The place had been one of considerable importance to the rebels, who had repaired and even partially manufactured their steamboat-navy there. Little or no injury appeared to have been done to the works or buildings by the retreating Johnnies; and our soldiers soon set things running again.

Moving up in the wood, half a mile or so from the river, our regiment proceeded to clear off a place for camp, with the rest of the brigade. The shanties were of course appropriated as officers' quarters; but the camping-ground was excellent; and by the help of shades made of boughs and brush, we soon had things fixed quite comfortably for the some what lengthened stay which we expected. This part of the country being comparatively uninjured by the war, there was of course considerable forage to be obtained; and our boys could not justly be accused of neglecting any opportunities, though the strictness of the orders from division head-quarters soon prevented any foraging to amount to any thing.

When soldiers camp in the wood in Summer, and expect to stay some time, as we did here, it is amusing to see what improvements they will make. In a little while our whole camp-ground was nicely cleared off, streets laid out, ample shades put up, wells dug, and preparations made for as much comfort as possible. The band-quarters were even nicer than usual. The boys had set their dog-tents in a row, on light walls of boards and stakes to make them higher; had built a long and heavy booth over the whole of them, dug a well and covered it, made themselves tables and seats in the shade, and even started a barber-shop, with a sign made of a piece of cracker-box badly lettered with shoe-blacking. The impression had now become pretty general that the war was over, and that we would probably stay here until ordered to Mobile for muster-out. Hoping this, and half-believing it, we felt like making the interim endurable as might be. But there were two or three companies who thought they hardly "got the worth of their money," when they kept details laboring faithfully for several days at digging a good, large well, and got it down some twenty or thirty feet, without finding water, when the order came to move. So calculations in the army, as elsewhere, prove very uncertain, though disappointment does not often have as pleasant a flavor as it did in this particular instance.

The colored people seemed to have heard of the "good time coming;" and from all the country round they flocked to our lines. For the first two or three days after our arrival, flat-boat after flat-boat came floating down the river to us, laden with negro-men, women and children, pigs, chickens, bed-clothes, rags and tatters, dirt and all, crowded and piled in promiscuous confusion. These people did not have the air of being as badly treated at home, as those of most other places we had seen; but they still had some idea of freedom and the Yankees, and were willing to risk themselves in trying them. It must be confessed that the reception they met, was not always such as to impress them favorably toward either freedom or the soldiers. Our regiment generally stood among the best in point of civility and kindliness to all; but there were some among us, even mean enough to "take" chickens from these poor creatures, who had thus come among us helpless, and so nearly destitute. The negroes, *en masse*, were provided for, probable as well as the post quarter-master could do under the circumstances; but the unaccustomed roughness of military treatment, though meant in kindness, must have seemed to them in many cases, harder than their accustomed ill-usage at home.

On the 28th, the news reached us of the surrender of Dick Taylor's army—the last organized force of rebels east of the Mississippi. We heard it with joy and thankfulness. The war was now surely over, at least on land, and east of the great river. But the rebel fleet which had gone up the Tombigbee, was still above us, and it was our business to be ready for their coming down. A large fort was planned, on the bank of the river, in such a way as to fully command its passage; and work on it had already been commenced. The saw-mill was pushed to the hardest to get the necessary lumber ready; and heavy fatigue-details were kept at work to build the fort. It was to be an honor to all concerned. But, things did not get ahead fast. The men all believed that the war was over, and the fort would never be of any use; and so they would not work, and could not be made to work. All ways of detailing were tried, from the usual squad from each company, up to a whole regiment, colonel and all; but still the fort would not grow very much. It lacked the pressure of apparent reason. One regiment at Spanish Fort would throw up more dirt in a single night, than all the details did here, in all the time of our stay.

So the days passed—work and rest alternating, but work having greatly the advantage. Saturday morning, the 6th of May, a boat came up the river with a load of paroled prisoners from Lee's army. In a little while, the news spread that the rebel fleet above us, was to come down soon, surrendered, and we were to go with it to Mobile. Great was the cheering and jubilation; for going to Mobile, then seemed to us to be surely the first step for home. Next morning, at a quarter after eight, the first boat of the rebel fleet, came in sight; and as her side swung round so that the name "*Jeff. Davis*" could be read, she was greeted with a cheer from the crowd that gathered on the shore. We would indeed have been very glad to meet the original Jeff. under similar circumstances.

By the next morning, the whole rebel fleet had arrived, with one or two exceptions. Here now was food for curiosity. Here were two of the gun-boats which had thrown "railroad freight-trains" at us, at Spanish Fort; here was the little, black tow-boat-looking craft, yclept the *Diamond*, which had once been rigged out as a gun-boat, by the rebel ladies of Alabama, who had given up even their ear-rings and other jewels for its preparation; and perhaps, even a greater curiosity to us, was the low, rakish-built blockade-runner *Heroine*, with its peculiar wheels, and its alleged powers of running eighteen miles an hour. What scenes had not these boats been through! and what romance might be written of them! They were ours now; and into the hands of our division, this last and most important naval surrender seemed now to be made. Some amusement, by the way, was occasioned by the finding, on one of the boats, of a tin sign, emblazoned in large, gilt letters, with the words "Taylor never surrenders."

The rebel officers commanded much attention, from the portly Commodore Farrand, with the handsome woman in black who was currently reported to be his mistress, down to the youngest and smallest of the grey-backed and gold-laced gentry. The peaceable sight of rebel officers was not then as common to us as it afterward became. Before the boats had all arrived, details for work on the fort had been discontinued by order of the division-commander in person. Spades suddenly stuck fast in the ground, and picks were at a sudden discount. Fort something-or-other, which was to have been an honor to the gallant General, &c., &c., was *mortum in embryo*. The General said there must be wood enough cut to run the boats down to Mobile, and we would go as soon as that was done. In a little while the whole wood rang with the sound of axes; and if ever four-foot-wood was cut and piled up faster, it must have been because there were more men to do it.

At last the welcome order came for the start. Never were knapsacks packed more cheerfully than on this morning of the 9th of April. We had reveille at half-past three, were ready to move at five, started about nine, turned back, started again, stacked arms and waited a long time on the bank of the river; and at last embarked. Seven companies and head-quarters of the regiment went on board the *Magnolia*; and the remaining companies on another boat. At half-past twelve the signal-gun was fired; the various bands of martial-music, and one brass band belonging to the division, sent out their most lively strains; and the fleet started off in due line and order down the river. Good-bye, navy-yard; and ho! for Mobile.

CHAPTER XXII.

DELAY AND DISAPPOINTMENT.

The trip down the Tombigbee river seemed to us but preparatory to that long-hoped-for one which should take us up the Mississippi to our homes. But we soon found to our sorrow, that "there's many a slip 'twixt the cup and lip;" and many a weary day would roll around ere we could finally turn our faces homeward. Day-light had come, indeed, but the sun-rise was not yet near. We reached Mobile at 8 o'clock on Tuesday evening, and after a delay of two or three hours, marched out north of the city, to find a place for camp. This was by no means a cheerful time. Though the distance was only three miles, it seemed nearer a dozen. The dismal swamp over whose dreary length we had to pass, was resonant with the doleful croak of frogs innumerable, and every one of them, to our imaginative ears, seemed to call the name of our brigade-commander. "K-r-e-e-etz, K-e-e-e-e-tz" they sang, and a hundred or so of voices in the regiment would echo it in a little more intelligible English, but with even more doleful emphasis and drawl, as they thought of the frogs and King Stork in the fable.

Camp was reached at last—a bare and comfortless place, on which we merely tumbled down to sleep as best we could. Next day our regimental-commander found an excellent place for us, near the bank of the river, and within the lines of some old earth-works about three miles above town. Here, under the shade of the noble trees, we cleared off and fixed up a neat, well-arranged and comfortable camp. On the 11th we drew eight months' pay, and settled clothing account for the second year. This made us rich; but our jollity had an off-set in the report that we were to go to Texas. Kirby Smith, it seemed, refused to surrender; and we were to help convince him of the necessities of the case. This was a terrible draw-back to our comfort. What reason or justice was there in it? There were plenty of veteran troops in the army; why could they not go, if any had to, and let us go home as we ought? And so the time passed, between hope and fear, till the worst was finally known.

Mobile soon became a familiar place to us. Nominally, there were all the restrictions upon leaving camp, but practically few of the men stopped to ask many questions when they wanted to go. In a day or two, the boys had gathered so many skiffs and canoes from the different wharves in town, that there was a regular fleet of them. Regularly every morning, the whole collection would be manned by soldiers who wanted to go to town. It was but a pleasant row down the river; and for the return-trip the wind generally blew, so that a few leafy boughs, erected as sails, would quickly and easily waft the little fleet home.

The city was now full of rebels, paroled from Dick Taylor's army, who still retained their rebel uniform and opinions, and made no attempt at concealing either. They would talk freely, and with all boldness, generally seeming willing to acknowledge that they were whipped for the present, but confident of a more successful conflict with us in the future. Some were anxious to go over and join Kirby Smith. A few, perhaps, were willing to accept the logic of events, and settle down to quiet citizenship; but certainly, the greater number were rebellious as ever, and wholly unsubdued in thoughts and feelings.

We could not be in town all the time; and as there was now no duty to perform, the time hung slow and idle on our hands. With eight months' pay in their pockets, and nothing to occupy their minds, many of the boys soon got to gambling excessively. "Chuck-a-luck" banks were set up in the wood a few steps from camp, and surrounded all the time by crowds of eager players. The story was the same as in all such cases: the "luck" all gradually centered in a few, and these generally the ones who kept the banks. There were some who gained a considerable amount of money by their gambling, but by far the greater number lost the most of their wages. Starting, of course, among the lower and more ignorant of the soldiers, the excitement soon spread till it involved many who had usually been supposed to hold themselves far above any thing of the kind. Our regiment was not alone in the matter. The practice was universal. Every where, if there was a camp, there was gambling; and every where it was characterized by the same features. Much of the hard-won earnings of many a poor soldier went away from him at the rattling of the dice, while his family at home, hitherto so well remembered, were perhaps suffering for the help it should have given them. But gambling seemed epidemic, and reason in abeyance.

Of course, the mails now had even more than the usual interest for us; and certainly the folks at home, could not accuse us of neglecting them. At one time our regiment sent out five hundred and ninety-six letters, beside papers and parcels, in a mail that had been but three days in gathering. For some cause or other, rations were now better than usual;

and they seemed more abundant, because so many of the boys bought their own food. Perhaps our regiment was peculiar in this respect; but most of us seemed determined to have wholesome food, rather than army-rations alone, whenever we could get it; and at ten cents a pound for bread, and sixty cents for butter, with other things in proportion, of course, the money flowed freely away.

These now were days of suspense and doubt; of good news one hour, contradicted by bad the next; of rumors and counter-rumors; of hopes and fears. As to our future, there seemed to be a general state of "don't know." If any of the officers were better informed than the privates about it, they certainly had succeeded in acquiring unprecedented reticence. One day an order would come, such as to immediately start a report that we must soon go home; and the next, another order would give a sadly-contrary impression. We wished to shirk no duty, and never had shrunk from any thing required of us; but this prospect of being ordered to Texas, was one that the most patient could not cheerfully contemplate. We felt that we ought to be at home.

So the days wore on—days of rest, indeed, but weary with suspense and hope deferred. Lying dreaming, under the shady trees, we could look across the bay, in an afternoon, and see the red lines of Spanish Fort, marked distinctly in the sunshine; and as we remembered the long days of fatigue and danger there, and their relation to the present time and circumstances, we could not but wonder whether the next month, witnessing as great a change, should see us safe at home. Home, home! How dear the Northern Summer seemed to us, with its prairies that blossomed so peaceful and smiling; and how inexpressibly, tenderly dear those loved and loving hearts, that waited patiently and trustingly for our coming, and the fond eyes that would thrill us with their loving gaze, and the gentle fingers that would clasp our own! We had been absent long, in hardship and danger not less than others; had faithfully fulfilled our promises; and now we thought the end should come.

> "The light that shone in the soldiers' eye,
> Was a longing thought of home."

But the monotony of waiting was broken at last, by an event of the most terrible destruction, sudden and fearful to the city, as unexpected and overwhelming battle could have been to soldiers. At 3 o'clock in the afternoon of Thursday, the 25th of May, the ware-house in the northern suburbs of Mobile, which was used as a store-house for ammunition, and then contained many tons of shells, torpedoes, cartridges and powder, exploded, with a noise such as he might hear, who should be shot from a one-hundred-pound cannon. We, who were in camp, were perfectly astonished, but could not imagine the cause of the terrible sound. In a few seconds, the vast and majestic column of smoke that rolled slowly, curling and wreathing upward, told the nature of the explosion. The papers of the time, described the event as well as they could; but no words can convey an adequate idea of the ruin and devastation thus in a single second wrought. Those who saw it will never forget, and those who did not, càn never imagine the appearance of the city, after the catastrophe. It is not positively known that any of our regiment were injured by the explosion; but one member was never heard of afterward. Whether he was blown up, or drowned, or whether he took the occasion to desert, was never known.

On the 27th, the official report was received of the surrender of Kirby Smith. The war at last was over. Had the end come suddenly, our joy would have been extreme; but the steps, though so great, had been so gradual and successive that when the first was passed the rest seemed easy. The end was come; and we thanked God. Should we not soon be at home? The suspense had not long to last. Mysterious are the ways of military government. Ignorant of their groundlessness and injustice some times, we obey without a murmur, orders which, if we had more knowledge of the circumstances, would be met with just and indignant disobedience. Had we known at the time, the whys and hows of the order which sent us to Texas, it is possible that some men of the regiment would have been so reckless in their anger, that the General who gave the order, might in five minutes have repented of it to the end of his life.

For a number of days we were under orders to be ready to march at an hour's notice; and on the morning of the 31st the notice came. At two in the afternoon, we were on the move. Knowing it must be a sea-voyage which should take us to Texas, the boys had provided themselves with sacks and boxes of extra provisions, which, had the trip been a march, could not have been carried half a day. But ships will carry a great deal; and the only limit to each man's baggage seemed to be his ability to take care of it. Marching slowly and laboriously down to the city, we rested on a wharf till some time in the night; and then embarked on transports, which took us out to the good ship *Continental*, on which, with a part of another regiment, we stood out to sea. The smell of salt water was no more new to us; but it takes more navigation than we ever tried, to keep a landsman's stomach steady when the ship falls away from under him continually. Sea-sickness is nothing new, and needs no description here. Happy are they who have never known it!

With pleasant weather, a comparatively smooth sea, and no remarkable event on the way, except that no lives were lost from thus crowding human beings in a ship, like hogs in a slaughter-pen. The voyage passed quite monotonously; and the 6th of June found us off Brazos Island. Months before, we had heard of this place as one of the worst where soldiers were ever stationed. It was said that they could not even have water to drink, except what was distilled from the sea. We had congratulated ourselves then, that duty had not called us there; yet here it was now before us, and we felt some what as the wicked may feel, who at the end of life have full belief in purgatory.

The channel at Brazos is so shallow that no ships drawing more than nine feet of water can safely pass. The troops were conveyed to the shore by a small steamboat used as lighter, which had to make several trips over the tossing waves to get a single ship unloaded. On one of these trips, those who were on board had perhaps a narrower escape from death than they had ever known in battle. The waves ran high; and the frail craft struck bottom several times so violently that the crew, and others who knew the danger, began to think their time had come. But here especially ignorance was bliss. Most of the men on board knew little of the danger until it was past. Nothing serious actually happened; and after a few more thumps the little steamer passed the bar, and soon reached the landing in safety. We were glad enough to set foot on land again, bare sand though it was; but even the land seemed rolling and tumbling occasionally, as bad as the unstable billows; and it was some time before this feeling wore away. The dangers of the deep were over for the present, but comfort was no nearer.

CHAPTER XXIII.

THE HOUR IS ALWAYS DARKEST THAT IS JUST BEFORE DAY.

The island which bears the euphoneous Spanish name of Brazos de Santiago, is a low, flat, sandy place, but a few feet out of water; and among its greatest faults is the fact that it is out of water at all. General Taylor's army had gathered here, before the invasion of Mexico; and from the observatory on the flag-staff in front of head-quarters, could be seen with a glass his old battle-fields of Point Isabel and Palo Alto, while Resaca de la Palma was almost in sight. There were men in our regiment who had been here in his army; but the memory of those days was very little help to them now. However, if his army could stand it, we could.

We were here now as part of General Steele's army of occupation, which, hastily thrown together, had not yet been duly sub-divided and organized. Our brigade-organization had been partially retained, but beyond that there was little definiteness. Orders for a small detail for fatigue-duty would come some times to the regiment direct from head-quarters of the army. Except the necessary fatigue and guarding of camp, there was no duty to be done; and to merely exist between the blazing sun and an oven of hot sand, with no protection from the one, but the little dog-tents, and no screen from the other, but such bits of boards and wooden boxes as could be gathered and saved among so many men, was the round of the monotonous days. A salt-water bath occasionally lent variety; but there were sharks in those waters, and it was unsafe to venture far from shore.

On the eastern side of the island, where we were now camped, there had for some time been a small military station. A regiment of negroes was now on duty as garrison; and their daily guard-mounting and parade were objects of much attraction to us, their proficiency in drill being the greatest we had ever seen. The whole regiment would go through the bayonet-exercise with more uniform accuracy than any single company of white troops in our knowledge. Whatever else may be affirmed of the negroes, it need not to us be denied that they made excellent soldiers. As guards, where white people also are concerned, they are not the most agreeable, on account of too literal and unreasoning obedience to orders.

Near the landing, a number of small frame buildings had been erected by the Government, and were used as head-quarters, ware-houses, offices, hospital, &c. The condensing apparatus, by which all the fresh water used there was distilled from the sea, consisted of four steam engines, located in a building near the water's edge, and having suitable tanks to hold the nauseous fluid as it was manufactured. As the vile but precious stuff was issued only in scanty rations, there must of course be a constant guard over the tanks lest it should be stolen. The negroes were kept on this duty; and their unreasoning fidelity to the literal words of their orders, with their inability to read any writing presented to them, were the cause of much inconvenience, and came near resulting in some individual collisions.

The ration of water issued to the troops was at first a gallon daily to each man—the whole allowance, for all purposes. The amount proved too great for the capacity of the condensers; and on the 11th, the allowance was cut down to a half-gallon per day to each. It may be supposed that this was scanty enough; but this was but a part of the discomfort. The water had to be drawn daily, like other rations; and there was almost nothing to keep it in. Canteens, kettles, and every thing else were put to more use than ever before. Hastily thrown together, in a strange country, and under strange circumstances, the army had but few conveniences; and the belief, which had gained ground, that we would not be retained much longer in the service, had bred a slackness in feeling and discipline that would have greatly impaired the efficiency of any detail, and which by no means added to the comfort of the regiment, It was probably the fault of circumstances rather than of persons.

The scarcity of water was now such as could not long be endured. On the 14th our regiment, with nearly all the others, was ordered to Clarksville, opposite Bagdad, in Mexico, near the mouth of the Rio Grande, and some nine miles west of Brazos. Here was plenty of fresh water, such as it was. The Rio Grande is a very swift and muddy stream; and its water now looked like very strong coffee into which some generous woman had put the milk and sugar—but it didn't taste that way, to any remarkable extent. If an ordinary bucket was filled with it and left to stand over night, in the morning the water would be found clear and beautiful, with a sediment of mud two inches deep at the bottom. So purified, it was excellent to drink; and even fresh from the river it was better than the distilled water at Brazos, which always had a sickish taste, and was peculiarly calculated to upset the epigastric gravity.

Bagdad would doubtless have been a beautiful city if the site were better, and there had been plenty of nice buildings there. As it is, however, it is a wretched and dirty place; but those who have worn shoulder-straps long enough to know, assert that its like is not to be found, as a place wherein to get some thing good to drink. At first, wonderful bargains were to be had there in goods. Our boys would go over, either with or without a pass, some times by swimming the river, change a few greenbacks for gold with some broker on the street, and buy clothing for the happy days when every man should be a citizen. There were probably few among us who did not thus obtain some memento of Bagdad, and win at the same time the distinction of having been to Mexico.

Between living on a red-hot sand-bar at Brazos, and the same thing at Clarksville—as the place was called, where once a few houses may have stood—the difference, except as to the water, was mostly in name. Existence became more like that of the animals than ever before; for in other places we generally either had some thing to do, or could do some thing. But here, what could be done? The heat was excessive, though there was always a strong breeze. For fuel, the dependence was on the drift-wood which had floated down the river, and been washed on shore by the waves of the gulf. For a day or two, while the novelty lasted, there was much interest in the view of the French fleet and other vessels, lying off the mouth of the river; in aquatic exercises in the surf; and in the strange appearance, desolate as it was, of the country generally; but this did not last long. A soldier of three years' experience, can exhaust the novelty of a place in a very little while.

Clear down there, almost out of the world, as it seemed to us—and certainly out of the best part of it—we felt as if cut off from civilization. A good, heavy mail from home would have been more than ever welcome—and at last it came. General Weitzel and his corps of Africanos arrived the same day, but that did not seem an event of half so much importance. Yet it was to us the dusky herald of the morning. On the afternoon of Saturday, the 24th of June, unexpected as an angel's visit, and more like that than any thing else, we as soldiers had ever known, came the order that the 33d Iowa Infantry was to be as soon as possible, mustered out of the service. If bad news flies like the wind, good news some times seems to spread instantaneously. When the order was known in camp, there was such joy as only they can guess, who have had a similar experience, and it expressed itself in tumultuous cheers and jubilation.

Tuesday morning, the 27th, we marched down to the landing at the eastern side of the island, to be ready to embark for Galveston. The day was excessively hot; and this last march of ours was one of the hardest we ever had. Many were compelled to lag behind, unable to move so fast over the scorching and yielding sand. But if guns and knapsacks and cartridge-boxes moved heavily, hearts were lighter than ever; for we were going home! But the winds and the sea were against us. A heavy surf had been for some days rolling. The steamer *Louise*, which had been running as a lighter, had gone out just before we reached the landing; and we were therefore compelled to wait, though every minute of delay was hard to bear. Next day at eleven we went on board the *Louise* and started; but the sea was too rough, and we had to turn back again. Thursday was no better. Would we never get started? The order would be countermanded before we could get beyond its reach.

On Friday there was some hope; but in the afternoon a regular "Northeaster" wind and storm arose, which tore up the waves tumultuously, and seemed scarcely likely to leave the land. Lumber-piles tumbled, tents turned summersaults, and valuable papers from the Quarter-master's office were scattered like forest leaves. It was well for us we were not on the gulf. The sand-bank of Brazos was bad enough, but any thing immovable was better than that world of treacherous, tossing waves in such a storm. That night there was a heavy rain. The flat sand of the island was all the time soaked so full of water, that the rain fell almost as on a floor. In the morning, the whole eastern end of Brazos was very nearly an unbroken sheet of water. Thank Providence! it was our last night on the island.

At a quarter after eleven A. M., of Saturday, July 1st, we again went on board the *Louise*, and started, this time for good. "The breaking waves dashed high," but we passed safely through the channel. The boat could not come any where near the ship *Warrior*, on which we were to embark, so a couple of Mexican schooners were used as lighters; and at last, after much difficulty and some danger, we found ourselves and our baggage safely on board the ship, and under way for Galveston. Farewell forever, Brazos de Santiago; and may our worst enemy never see thee!

The *Warrior* was a good, strong ship, sure though slow. We had plenty of room, and nothing to do but hope. Nothing remarkable happened. A sea-voyage at best is monotonous: what must it be, then, to a regiment of soldiers, without reading matter, and without any accommodations but those their own ingenuity devised? The sea was not very rough; but the ship rolled considerably. The Chaplain's face became as that of a man who has lost all that makes life desirable; and he was not alone in his misery. There were more pale and sorrowful countenances among us than there would have been on land if we had been going to our own funerals. At about 8 P. M., of Monday, we entered the port of Galveston, and reported for further orders. Compelled to wait for the tide till next morning, we made the best of the opportunities the town afforded, among which were the most excellent water-melons our eyes had ever seen.

The morning of the 4th was clear and beautiful. We were awakened by the lively music of a brass band in town, accompanied by a salute from a battery of field artillery. The 4th of July was being celebrated, even here in Texas, though probably none of the citizens showed any sign of participation. What must have been their feelings, as they reflected that now, for the first time in four years, the cannon roared in honor of the day, in every State and Territory of the Union! Our ship moved out at about five in the morning; and as we passed the U. S. fleet, which guarded the entrance to the bay, the gunboats and some of the ships, were gaily decorated with flags, looking jubilant and patriotic, as a delegation of uniformed girls, at a Sunday School celebration. As for us, we sped on homeward, and thought of the "4ths" we had seen, and of those yet to come.

At half past-five of Wednesday afternoon, we entered the South-west Pass of the Mississippi, and thankfully saw our last of salt water. It was joy indeed to see again the noble river; and our eyes rested with delight upon the greenness of the grass and weeds that fringed its banks. It was now a month since we had seen any vegetation, except the little at Galveston. But there is no rose without its thorn. With the fresh water came the mosquitos, swarms and myriads, murdering peace and sleep. At eleven we reached quarantine, and were compelled to lie over till next morning, though the delay was miserably irksome.

Thursday forenoon, among the new and welcome scenery of the ever-varying banks of the river, was a school-house — a regular school-house — strange sight to us in those days! A white lady officiated as teacher, and a whole tribe of little darkey children were the scholars, the entire crowd of whom rushed out of doors as we passed, and cheered and shouted welcome. This was the first greeting on our homeward way; and the incident gave cause for thought. Passing the wreck of the rebel gun-boat *Webb*, which had so boldly, recklessly run past our fleets and batteries on the way down from Red river, we came on, slowly but surely, toward the goal of our immediate hopes; and at half-past twelve we entered New Orleans. The city seemed familiar, though our acquaintance with it was so little. We looked across at our former camping-ground at Algiers, but we cared little for it now; our thoughts were of home.

By Friday noon a place was found for us to land; but before we could get to shore the ship had to wander up and down along the levee, very much as the old *Izetta* did when we were there before. Disembarking at last, we were marched to the old "Alabama Cotton-press," on Tchoupitoulas street, at the corner of Robin — one of a number of large, deserted warehouses in that vicinity. Here was abundance of room for our regiment, with such accommodations as would have seemed exceedingly comfortable in the earlier part of our soldiering.

Now came days of unavoidable delay, while the papers were being made out for our discharge. Soon there was a scene of more literary activity, than our regiment had ever known. All the tables on the premises were appropriated, and new ones improvised; and pens and ink were in unprecedented demand. All the best penmen in the ranks had to suffer for their skill, by detail to help make out the muster-rolls. In justice to the officers, it must be said that they seemed anxious as any, to hasten the day of discharge. "Many hands make light work;" and so the multitudinous rolls which red-tape requires, before it will say to the waiting soldier "Depart in peace," were prepared with cheerfulness and speed.

But there was sadness among the recruits, whose term of service would not expire soon enough to let them out with the rest. They had the express understanding, when they enlisted, that they were to be mustered out with the regiment; and there was much feeling among them, when the order came now for their transfer to the 34th Iowa. One or two desertions took place among them. The recruits left us on the 13th of July. How much justice there was in their feelings against the officers who recruited them, will not be investigated here. They did not lose as much by the transfer, as was expected, for the 34th was before a great while, mustered out.

As the time drew near for our starting North, our interest in the dry-goods market increased. Citizens' clothing came greatly in fashion; and there were few who did not lay in at least a partial supply. The benefit of new clothes were never more observable. Private soldiers Tom, Dick and Harry, laid aside their ragged uniform, and became Messrs. Thomas, Richard and Henry. And so the change from soldiering to citizenship came gradually. At last the probation ended; the last paper was finished, the arms turned over, the formalities concluded. The discharges which had been all made out, were sent to the mustering-officer, who signed them and returned them, when they were packed with other regimental-documents in a box, and placed in charge of Major Boydston, till we should arrive at the place of final discharge. A little before noon of Tuesday, July 15th, we left the old press, and marched joyfully down to the levee. Of course, the worst and slowest boat in the city, had been provided for us, and on the old and rickety "*Sunny South*" we embarked, at half-past two in the afternoon. New Orleans was left behind; and we joyfully realized that now indeed, we were homeward bound.

CHAPTER XXIV.

HOME AGAIN.

The steamer *Sunny South* on which we were to ascend the Mississippi, was but a little craft; but we who were mustered out were not a whole regiment. Even if the crowding and discomfort had been manifold worse we should have felt cheerful and jolly; for the end was nigh. Every boat on the river passed us, and vexed us with every new comparison of delay; but still we bore along. At a quarter after nine next morning we reached Baton Rouge, touched at Port Hudson at 1:15, rounded to at Morganza Bend at five P. M., and reached Natchez at seven in the evening. Here the old scow had to stop and repair her boilers. Friday, we still lived; and at 5:15 in the afternoon the *Sunny South* tied up at Vicksburg. She was now pronounced unsafe; and we were therefore transferred to another boat—the *W. H. Osborne*—which, though not the fastest craft in the world, was roomy, clean and comfortable.

If one would form an idea of the greatness of this country, let him take such a trip as ours, from Brazos to Davenport. Accustomed all our lives to think of New Orleans as down South away toward the tropics, we had found ourselves going some three hundred miles northward to that city, and then commencing a steamboat ride of eighteen hundred miles on a single river to our northern homes. On Sunday evening, before sun-down we reached the mouth of the Yazoo Pass. Every eye was turned with memory's deepest interest to this scene of the beginning of our first expedition. But its appearance was changed since then; and what was deep water when we passed through the channel, was now dry land. It was dark when we touched at Helena, but the outlines of the place, though changed, were still familiar. How the tide of memories rolled over us, as now, homeward bound, our term of service out at last, safe and whole and hopeful, we looked back upon the time when these hills and hollows of Helena were a present reality to us, and all the joy we now felt was then but a dream of the uncertain future!

It was but a little thing, yet it seemed a curious coincidence that among the passengers with us on the boat, was a man who had been a rebel Colonel at Fort Pemberton, on the Yazoo, when our forces attacked that position. He was quite talkative and companionable; and conversation with him gave an inside view of the conflict there, to balance the outside one of our own experience. Would all the rebel South prove courteous as he, that vanquished and victors should ever together talk over their battles, and thus in admiration of each other's courage lose the bitterness of the feeling which nerved them to the fight? Would it might be so!

One phenomenon which we noticed, seemed strange to us: On the morning of Tuesday, the 25th, the river where we were appeared to be rather low; and the boat took occasional soundings. By night, however, we found the river high, and frequently out of its banks. This may be nothing remarkable to men of more experience on the Mississippi, but to us it seemed strange. At a little after six P. M., of Tuesday, we reached Columbus, Kentucky, where our first real soldiering occurred; and at half-past nine, the lights of Cairo were before us. It had been our confident expectation, to leave the river here, and take the cars for Davenport; but there was no transportation ready for us, and so we were doomed to boat it the rest of the way. When this was known, there was cursing and gnashing of teeth. Many, who could not endure the prolonged suspense of the steam-boat passage, got off at Cairo, and procured their own transportation by railroad. As every day's travel brought us nearer home, the days and miles seemed to lengthen almost intolerably; and every minute's delay was noticed and irksome.

After reaching Cairo, we felt as though we were on free soil again, for the first time in almost three years. Yet there was little more appearance of welcome, than had greeted us hundreds of miles farther South; for all the way was much the same in this respect. As the boat passed houses along the banks, doors flew open, windows sprang up, kerchiefs fluttered, and the voices of children rang out the shout of greeting. At one place there was an especial expression of enthusiasm: A little crowd of women and children was gathered in front of a house as we passed, and their joy showed itself even more exuberantly than usual. They waived their bonnets, kerchiefs, aprons, or whatever else they happened to have in hand, and one woman, unable to get hold of any thing else in the excitement of the moment, enthusiastically waived her baby. The novel greeting was acknowledged by a shout and much good-humored laughter.

At 8 o'clock of Thursday morning, we reached St. Louis; and now came a "realizing sense" that we were indeed, going home. Our regiment was transferred to the steamer *Muscatine;* and at 4:30 in the afternoon, we were again on the move. The river was much obstructed by drift-wood, and the boat very heavily loaded. Vexed as we had been by delays and slowness, every slackening of speed was noticed. "Making eight hours a mile," the boys would cry. "Who kicked the boat?" the boys would halloo, when the speed was suddenly accelerated a little. Little Sergeant Crow, would stand on the bow of the boat, and make piteous appeals to the engineer not to run so fast and take away his breath.

The repeated soundings vexed the boys. "N-o bot-tom" had been heard so often, in all the drawling and unearthly tones that could be imagined, that we were sick of it. "N-o-o bottom—quarter past twain—no bottom, *scant*," and so on, with all possible varieties, the lead-man's calls were echoed. River captains are always careful to keep their boats trim as possible, by having the weight evenly adjusted, so that the boat will set right on the water. Soldiers are always crowding to one side or the other; and thus the officers of the boats are always in trouble—some times, we thought, too much so. "Oh! Captain," some one called out to the short but portly Captain L——, who was standing on the bow, very near the center of the boat, and looking to one side, "Oh! Captain, turn round; they want to trim the boat," and some of the boys asserted that the fat engineer kept walking from side to side, to preserve the balance.

At a little after 9 o'clock on the morning of Saturday, the 29th of July, our hearts thrilled within us, at the first sight of Iowa. Always proud as we were of the State, it had never seemed so dear to us as now. Here were our loved ones, waiting to welcome us. Hail, Iowa! ever in the van of Freedom, proud among the proudest, young, beautiful and strong! Three years out of our lives, we had given to the country's cause; here now was home again, with its peace and rest. Hail Iowa! As we rounded to at Keokuk, a brass band on a steamer lying at the levee, struck up its liveliest notes, a lot of ladies standing near, waved their kerchiefs, and smiled and looked eloquent welcome, and every body seemed as glad to see us as though we had all been born and raised in the place. Col. Mackey called for "Three cheers for old Iowa," and they rang out loud and hearty, from every blue-coated and true-hearted man of us—three cheers, and with a will. So our first greeting in the State, though unheralded and accidental, was hearty and sincere, as the patriotism of the city, that in the beginning of the war, had at a moment's notice, repeatedly improvised and sent out company after company to aid the Union cause, when the rebels grew troublesome in North-East Missouri.

A number of the boys went on shore at Keokuk, and stayed so long that the boat went off and left them. In some cases, this would be a very uncomfortable circumstance to the parties concerned; but it proved of very little consequence to them, for they merely walked up the railroad track, along the river twelve miles, to Montrose, waited there till the boat came up, and then came on it again. Reaching Muscatine next day, we thought the place seemed remarkably still and lifeless. The stores were closed, and the streets deserted. What could be the matter? We could hardly buy even a few apples. It seemed very odd to us; and it was some time before we happened to remember that the day was Sunday, and we were now in the North. Down where we had been, Sunday was just like any other day, "only a little more so;" and the difference now was very plainly noticed.

At noon that day we reached Davenport. Here our coming was known. There was quite a little crowd of ladies and gentlemen gathered on the levee; but the only word or sign of welcome that greeted us as we touched the landing was the voice of an officer on shore shouting to our Colonel, "Don't let a man get off! Don't let a man get off!" If this had been the spirit of the State, we would have turned our backs on Iowa; and we could not but contrast this greeting with that of Keokuk, and remember that even the negro children in the South, had many times been more glad to see us than our own fellow-citizens here in a city which expected to receive all the benefits that could accrue to the place of our muster-out. There was not one of us but remembered it, and will remember it when more important matters are forgotten.

Crossing the river immediately, we landed on the island, and marched up to the camp formerly occupied by rebel prisoners. Here, among the numerous buildings on the north side of the yard, we found comfortable quarters, and taking possession of them, set ourselves to endure the waiting for the paymaster and our discharges. The grounds were beautiful for a camp; and we could have been well content to remain there several months, had the time been taken from the other end of our term of service. As it was, the delay was most irksome and intolerable. It was mere waiting, without occupation, and with one great, absorbing thought and feeling, too prominent to admit any thing else. Discipline was at an end. Even the rations were drawn by voluntary fatigue-parties. Had there been an attempt made to draw a detail from the regiment for any duty, it would have been difficult to gather a dozen men. Fortunately there were no orders given, and scarcely any appearance of authority was continued. The *esprit de corps* was gone, and every one seemed absorbed in his own individual going home.

Previous regiments, upon discharge at Davenport, had made great disturbance, and "played smash" generally; and it was the fear of this from us that sent us over to the Island. But our men roamed free and undisturbed, and no complaint whatever was brought against them. Respecting themselves and others, they behaved like gentlemen, and were complimented therefor in Davenport as well as elsewhere.

If one should have asked us, during the first two or three days of our stay on the Island, what we noticed most in Iowa, the answer most probably would have been different from what he might have expected; for we should have answered, without hesitation, that it was the good looks of the ladies. It is but reasonable to suppose that perhaps we were some what prejudiced in their favor; and some thing is doubtless due to the fact that they did not meet us on the streets with averted eyes, and rebel thoughts and feelings manifest in every feature, as did those to whom we had become most accustomed; but it can not be denied that with at least equal ease and grace of manner, the Northern ladies, in all that the appearance of youth and health, rosy cheeks, sparkling eyes, elastic tread, and cheerful, buoyant intelligence of expression can add to female beauty and attractiveness, have greatly the advantage of the sallow, listless and puny-looking ladies who had been visible to us in the Southern cities; and we could not but frequently notice the difference with admiration. All the ladies we saw now seemed good-looking, and most of them decided beauties.

Seven days we were kept waiting at Davenport for our pay and discharges—seven long, weary days, all the longer and more weary for our being so near home. Had we been a thousand miles away, we could have endured the waiting better; but to be so near home, and hindered so outrageously, as many if not most of us believed, by mere collusion among officials and interested parties, was almost torture. Very likely the officers in charge of the matter may have done the best they could; but there were few of us who thought so.

At last the eventful day came. At 9 o'clock on the morning of Tuesday, the 8th of August, the long expected pay-master came over from town; and our heart thrilled with the feeling that now in a few minutes we should be citizens again, free, and equal. Colonel Mackey called the regiment together *en masse*, without any attempt at military order, and addressed to them the following brief farewell:

"OFFICERS AND SOLDIERS: The time has arrived for the 33d regiment of Iowa Volunteer Infantry to disband. In taking leave of you as your commander, permit me to tender you my kindest regards for the treatment I have received from you during three years of active service. That I have committed errors in the discharge of my duties, I am fully aware; but I trust you will have charity enough to charge them to mistaken judgment. I have endeavored since I have been with you to discharge my duties toward you and our Government as well as I knew how. The best interest of the service, and your own personal welfare, have been my constant aim.

Your courage, industry and patriotism, it is not for me to extol. Of all these you have given ample proof on many well-fought fields; the suffering necessarily incident to three years' campaigning, the impartial historian must give you credit for well enduring; and a grateful people will receive and bless you as their defenders.

You entered the service in the darkest and most gloomy hour of our country's history. You have helped dispel that darkness and gloom, and now return to your homes, with your country at peace with the world, the unholy and unnatural rebellion, that was organized to crush this noble Republic, brought to a final and glorious end, and the integrity and stability of the Government fully vindicated. For all this you have great cause to rejoice and be thankful.

But in your rejoicing do not forget that many of the brave men who went out with us are not here for muster-out. They have sealed their patriotism with their lives, and have been offered up as a sacrifice on the altar of their country. Reserve a place in your hearts to cherish their memories; and let their little ones be your special care.

In retiring to private life, each and every one of you carries with him my warmest wishes for his success. Be as good citizens as you have been soldiers—and I have no doubt you will and your country-men will still have greater cause to be proud of you.

The privations and perils through which we have passed together, have endeared you all to me; and notwithstanding we separate here to join our families and friends, from whom we have been so long absent, the thought that we shall meet no more together, until the Reveille of Eternity shall be sounded, brings with it feelings of sadness, feelings which I have not words to express.

Officers and soldiers, as your colonel and commander, I bid you farewell!"

This parting word was received in respectful silence. It might be supposed that there came now a pathetic scene—that the men who had fought side by side so long, would not disband without some sign of sorrow; but such was not the case. We were to lose our organization, indeed, but would mostly be neighbors still; and even had not the hopes of happy meetings soon, to come with loved ones dearer far, been uppermost in every mind, Western men are made of too stern stuff to show much emotion at such a parting. Practically, the scene was the very reverse of pathetic. Each man, as his name was called, stepped to the window, received his greenbacks and discharge, and went forth, free and uncontrolled, whithersoever he pleased, hardly escaping the pleasant banter of those whose turn had not yet come. "How are you, citizen?" "Say, over yonder is Davenport. Do you think you can find the way, now that you have no body to take care of you?" There was much squaring-up of little debts, some hand-shakings and words of parting, from those who did not expect soon to meet again, and then each one, without waiting for the rest, took his individual way westward; and thus unceremoniously, the 33d Iowa Infantry disbanded.

The great majority of the men reached their homes on the night of the 9th — as nearly as could be, three years from the time of their enlisting. Thus had been answered the prayer and prophecy of that dear old song which had so often cheered us in the gloomiest hours:

"God bless you, boys! We'll welcome you home,
When rebels are in the dust!"

Who shall describe the sacred, sweet emotion of husband and wife, parent and son, so long parted, now met in happiness and home; or that newer, wilder rapture that thrilled the hearts of lovers, faithful still, joined now in an embrace whose exquisite bliss would gild all the past of trial and danger!

Home, home, home!
No more the deep-mouthed cannon's vengeful roar,
Or musket's rattling roll shall come,
No more, no more

No more the warning cry,
"Halt! who comes there?" — the watchful, straining gaze,
Shall warm the chilling blood with danger nigh,
In coming days.

No more the dull routine
Of camp, its weary drills and toilsome show —
Muster, parade, review — affect us now:
These all have been.

No more on burning sand,
Or through the gloomy swamp our course shall lay,
Where lurks the enemy on either hand,
By night or day.

No mcre the dreadful scene,
Of battle-field or hospital shall come
The happy dreams of future days between;
There's peace at home.

The weary night is past,
Oh! who shall tell the heart-felt happiness
Of this dear morning which in joy at last
Has come to bless?

APPENDIX

ROLL

OF THE

THIRTY-THIRD IOWA INFANTRY

COPIED FROM

REGIMENTAL DESCRIPTIVE BOOK

AT MUSTER-OUT.

FIELD AND STAFF OFFICERS.

MUSTERED IN.

SAMUEL A. RICE, Colonel. Promoted to Brigadier-General, August 4th, 1863.
CYRUS H. MACKEY, Lieut.-Colonel. Promoted to Colonel, April 22d, 1864.
HIRAM D. GIBSON, Major. Resigned, April 22d, 1864.
F. F. BURLOCK, Adjutant. Discharged by promotion to another regiment.
HENRY B. MYERS, Quartermaster. Resigned, March 16th, 1864.
ARAD PARKS, Surgeon. Resigned, January 11th, 1864.
JOHN Y. HOPKINS, Assistant Surgeon. Promoted to Surgeon, July 29th, 1864.
WM. N. SCOTT, Assistant Surgeon. Resigned, December 24th, 1864.
ROBERT A. MCAYEALLY, Chaplain. Resigned, July 24th, 1863.
BARTHOLOMEW FRANKEN, Hospital Steward. Discharged by promotion April 28th, 1864.
EUGENE W. RICE, Quartermaster-Sergeant. Promoted to Quartermaster, April 10th, 1864.
SAMUEL B. EVANS, Commissary-Sergeant. Discharged by promotion, Dec. 30th, 1865.
JOHN F. LACEY, Sergeant-Major. Promoted to Lieutenant, April 16th, 1863.

MUSTERED OUT.

CYRUS H. MACKEY, Colonel. Wounded at Jenkins' Ferry, April 30th, 1864.
JOHN LOFLAND, Lieutenant-Colonel.
CYRUS B. BOYDSTON, Major.
CHARLES H. SHARMAN, Adjutant. Wounded at Helena, July 4th, 1863.
EUGENE W. RICE, Quartermaster.
FRANCIS M. SLUSSER, Chaplain.
JOHN Y. HOPKINS, Surgeon.
JOHN R. CRAWFORD, Sergeant-Major. Wounded and taken prisoner at Jenkins' Ferry, April 30th, 1864.
REUBEN WHITAKER, Hospital Steward.
CHARLES G. BENNETT, Quartermaster-Sergeant.
ALBERT G. BERKEY, Commissary-Sergeant.
A. F. SPERRY, Principal Musician.

CASUALTIES.

Company A.

Josiah F. Curtis, wounded at Helena.
Nathaniel H. Richardson, taken prisoner at Mark's Mills.
James A. Beaver, killed at Helena.
James T. Duncan, wounded and probably killed at Jenkins' Ferry.
David Forst, taken prisoner at Helena.
Alfred Hager, wounded at Jenkins' Ferry.
Hiram P. Henry, taken prisoner at Helena, and wounded at Jenkins' Ferry.
John S. Johnston, wounded at Jenkins' Ferry.
Wm. F. McKern, killed at Helena.
Milton Miner, taken prisoner at Helena.
Peter McKenney, killed at Helena.
John B. Nichols, taken prisoner at Helena.
Henry H. Reaves, wounded at Helena.
Jesse T. Sherwood, killed at Helena.
Jonathan S. Tindall, wounded at Jenkins' Ferry.
James H. Wycoff, killed at Helena.

Company B.

John R. Alsup, taken prisoner at Jenkins' Ferry.
Jas. H. Davis, " " on Yazoo Pass.
Dennis Decker, " " " " "
" " wounded and taken prisoner at Jenkins' Ferry.
Francis M. Dyer, " " " "
William Harris, wounded at Spanish Fort.
James B. Herrell, taken prisoner on Yazoo Pass.
John Lee, " " " " "
John Manefee, wounded at Helena.
Jacob Newkirk, killed at Helena.
George Payton, jr., taken prisoner on Yazoo Pass.
Hannibal Rogers, wounded and taken prisoner at Jenkins' Ferry.
Jefferson Utterback, taken prisoner on Yazoo Pass.
Francis M. Wertz, wounded at Jenkins' Ferry.
George W. Long, wounded at Spanish Fort.
John E. Nichols, wounded at Jenkins' Ferry.

Company C.

Joshua B. Wells, wounded at Jenkins' Ferry.
John F. Gaunt, " " " "
George G. Curry, taken prisoner at Helena.
Reuben Coomes, wounded at Helena and taken prisoner at Jenkins' Ferry.
Frederick Butler, taken prisoner at Helena.
James Adair, wounded " "
Henry Coomes, " " "
James E. Chick, taken prisoner " "
William Campbell, wounded at Spanish Fort.
Edward Currier, killed at Helena.

Robert W. B. Currey, wounded at Jenkins' Ferry
John Dove, " " " "
Joab Fox, killed at Helena.
James H. D. Goodman, taken prisoner at Helena.
Sanford Graham, wounded at Helena.
Thomas G. Gooden, wounded at Spanish Fort.
Edward Graham, killed at Jenkins' Ferry.
William H. Harris, killed at Jenkins' Ferry.
Oliver Johnston, killed at Helena.
George W. Lundy, taken prisoner at Helena.
Henry C. Ludington, killed at Helena.
William Osborn, wounded at Helena, and wounded at Jenkins' Ferry.
John R. Pilgrim, taken prisoner at Helena.
Samuel Ream, wounded at Jenkins' Ferry.
James B. Spain, wounded at Helena.
Robert Talbot, " " "
William Victor, taken prisoner at Helena.
William B. Walker, wounded at Jenkins' Ferry.
John B. Williams, killed at Helena.
Owen Bartlett, wounded at Jenkins' Ferry.
Mortimer Jackson, " " " "

Company D.

Jacob Houser, killed at Helena.
William Hilliard, taken prisoner at Helena.
John W. Jones, wounded and taken prisoner at Jenkins' Ferry.
Moses F. Atwood, wounded at Helena.
Edwin B. Batterson, killed at Helena.
Levi E. Brundage, " " "
William E. Boyer, taken prisoner at Helena.
Samuel H. Doughman, wounded at Jenkins' Ferry.
Samuel L. Deweese, " " " "
Abraham C. Hopkins, taken prisoner at Helena.
Morris A. Quaintance, wounded and taken prisoner at Jenkins' Ferry.
John H. Ramey, wounded at Helena.
David Adams, wounded at Jenkins' Ferry.
William Trobridge, wounded and taken prisoner at Jenkins' Ferry.
George R. Mitchell, wounded at Jenkins' Ferry.
William Thorp, " " " "

Company E.

John M. Finney, wounded at Jenkins' Ferry.
Marion Dunbar, taken prisoner at Mark's Mills.
Lewis H. Cochran, wounded at Jenkins' Ferry.
Amos Cornes, killed at " "
Benjamin Cruzen, killed at " "
Adam Eichelberger, wounded and taken prisoner at Jenkins' Ferry.
John B. Harris, wounded at " "
Anthony Hawk, wounded and taken prisoner at " "
Thomas H. Hinkle, killed at " "
Philander McMullen, wounded and taken prisoner at " "

Samuel S. Robertson, wounded at Jenkins' Ferry.
Levi Shaw, wounded at " "
John S. Wharton, wounded at Spanish Fort.
David G. Wilson, wounded at Jenkins' Ferry.
Willis S. Bird, " " " "
John H. Miller, " " " "
Wheeler Chadwick, wounded and taken prisoner at Jenkins' Ferry.
Joseph Redpath, wounded at " "
William J. Bowers, " " " "
James W. Grover, " " " "
Daniel Bacon, " " " "

COMPANY F.

Ashley A. Buckner, killed at Helena.
Abraham Day, wounded at Spanish Fort.
Francis M. Gibson, taken prisoner at Jenkins' Ferry.
Walker B. Gibson, wounded and taken prisoner at Jenkins' Ferry.
Samuel B. Montgomery, wounded at " "
John N. Miner, wounded at Helena.
Daniel McCreary, killed " "
Joseph T. Miller, " " "
Thomas Hillwell, " "
Jasper Skinner, killed at Jen s' Ferry.

COMPANY G.

Isaac N. Ritner, wounded at in's Ferry.
Nicholas Schippers, wounded by shwhackers on Arkansas River, January 28th, 1864.
Lucien Reynolds, wounded and taken prisoner at Jenkins' Ferry.
Klyn de Bruyn, taken prison " "
Tunis Blockland, killed at He a.
William H. H. Downing, take isoner at Helena.
Joseph W. Dungan, wounded panish Fort.
William O. Downes, wounded enkins' Ferry.
Jacob Miller, killed at Helen .
John Metz, wounded at Spanis ort.
John Niermeyer, wounded and ken prisoner at Jenkins' Ferry.
William P. Smiley, killed at He na.
George W. Towne, wounded and taken prisoner at Jenkins' Ferry.
Jacob Taylor, wounded at " "
Enos M. Woods, wounded near Camden, Ark., April 15th, 1864, and left prisoner at Camden.
Thomas D. Wallace, wounded at Jenkins' Ferry.
Daniel Wiser, taken prisoner at Mark's Mills.
Martin Walraven, wounded at Spanish Fort.
John Henry, wounded and taken prisoner at Jenkins' Ferry.

COMPANY H.

John Wightman, killed at Jenkins' Ferry.
Thomas J. Lawler, wounded at " "
James Garrett, " " " "

Clark Bevin, wounded and taken prisoner at Jenkins' Ferry.
William T. Dison, wounded at “ “
Dorman Hiner, wounded at Jenkins' Ferry.
William Goldthwait, wounded at Jenkins' Ferry.
David Holloway, wounded and taken prisoner at Jenkins' Ferry.
William R. Hoyt, wounded at “ “
Thomas Landry, wounded and taken prisoner at “ “
Allen A. McNeil, wounded at “ “
Marvin A. Peck, wounded and taken prisoner at “ “
William J. Parks, “ “ “ “ “ “ “
Joseph M. Roland, killed at “ “
William M. Rodman, wounded and taken prisoner at “ “
Philip Suitor, wounded and taken prisoner at “ “
Oliver Seaton, left as nurse at Camden.
George W. Shanafelt, killed at Jenkins' Ferry.
John Shoff, wounded at “ “
James D. Compton, wounded and taken prisoner at Jenkins' Ferry.
Owen P. McNeal, wounded at “ “

COMPANY I.

Hans Fergerson, taken prisoner at Jenkins' Ferry.
Oscar L. Jones, wounded at “ “
Joseph Brobst, wounded and taken prisoner at Jenkins' Ferry.
Peter A. Bonebrake, wounded at “ “
John Bruett, wounded and taken prisoner at Jenkins' Ferry.
William P. Funk, killed at Prairie de Ann, April 10th, 1864.
William Goff, wounded at Helena.
Eri Goodenough, wounded at Jenkins' Ferry.
John M. Henderson, killed at “ “
John M. McCleland, wounded at “ “
William H. Parker, “ “ “ “
Thomas Smith, taken prisoner at Helena.
George W. Stanfield, killed at Helena.
James W. Strong, wounded and taken prisoner at Jenkins' Ferry.
John S. Snyder, “ “ “ “ “ “ “
James I. Welch, killed at “ “
David T. Welch, taken prisoner at “ “
John Spohn, killed at Helena.
Smith Dunlap, wounded and taken prisoner at Jenkins' Ferry.
William G. Reed, wounded at “ “

COMPANY K.

Matthew D. Gilchrist, killed at Helena.
William R. Cowan, wounded at Jenkins' Ferry.
David T. Evans, “ “ “ “
Henry C. Haskell, wounded and taken prisoner at Jenkins' Ferry.
Francis M. Playle, “ “ “ “ “ “ “
John C. Roberts, wounded at “ “
George B. Stratton, wounded and taken prisoner at “ “
Alexander Jones, “ “ “ “ “ “ “
John W. Martin, wounded at “ “
James Windell, killed at “ “

William H. Withrow, wounded at Poison Springs, April 15th, 1864.
William H. Anderson, wounded at Poison Springs.
Enoch F. Henderson, wounded at Jenkins' Ferry.
Samuel H. Smith, wounded and taken prisoner at Jenkins' Ferry.
William H. Coleburn, " " " " " " "
John Burgess, wounded on Walnut Ridge, April 15th, 1864.
Ephriam Smith, killed at Jenkins' Ferry.

MISCELLANEOUS CASUALTIES.

Colonel Cyrus H. Mackey, wounded at Jenkins' Ferry.
Captain Andrew J. Comstock, Co. C, wounded and taken prisoner at Jenkins' Ferry.
Captain L. W. Whipple, Co. G, wounded at Helena.
Captain Paris T. Totten, Co. I, died of wounds received at Jenkins' Ferry.
Second Lieutenant Oliver J. Kindig, Co. C, wounded at Jenkins' Ferry.
Second Lieutenant Charles H. Sharman, Co. G, wounded at Helena.
Second Lieutenant Wilson De Garmo, Co. H, wounded at Jenkins' Ferry.
First Lieutenant Thomas R. Connor, Co. K, killed at Jenkins' Ferry.

ROSTER OF THE REGIMENT.

ROSTER OF THE REGIMENT.

COMPANY A.

CYRUS B. BOYDSTON, *Captain.*

S. S. PIERCE, *First Lieutenant.*

E. R. WOODRUFF, *Second Lieutenant.*

Adams, Edwin M.
Antrim, William
Auten, John B.
Auten, Thomas
Bishop, Abijah W.
Barnhill, Benjamin
Barnhill, James
Brown, George
Brown, Wilson L.
Breese, Isaac
Brewster, Henry D.
Bellamy, Samuel W.
Busenburgh, Daniel
Beaver, James A.
Burdick, George L.
Brooks, Peter
Baker, Justus C.
Brown, Francis H.
Brown, William D.
Cooper, James M.
Curtis, Joseph F.
Collins, Lodrick C.
Cooper, Ephraim
Chrisman, William T.
Chrisman, James H.
Chambers, Zephaniah
Chambers, William
Chambers, William R.
Craig, John
Cradick, William W.
Harned, Michael R.
Hammond, Henry J.
Hammond, Greenville C.
Hager, Alfred
Hunter, Joseph F.
Heaton, Samuel
Hiatt, Lewis
Hodges, Milton J.
Hodges, William W.
Henry, Hiram P.
Hicks, Robert
Hicks, James
Harding, Wm. H.
Inman, John
Ivey, George R.
Johnston, John S.
Jolliffe, Albert
Jeffers, John
Kendrick, Americus
Kendrick, John C.
Kennedy, John
Levan, Jacob
Leach, Vincent
McKinney, John
McGuire, William
McKein, Wm. F.
May, Alexander P.
Miner, Milton
Morrow, William J.
Moltern, Wm. J.
Rowland, David W.
Reaves, Henry H.
Reaves, Clark
Richards, Lorenzo D.
Roan, Nat. C.
Richards, John
Schee, Oliver
Sherwood, Jesse F.
Smith, Hamilton E.
Smith, George W.
Snyder, John
Shawver, Jacob
Sampson, Levi J.
Stone, Freeman M.
Shilling, John
Sturdefant, Thaddeus
Todd, Jacob P.
Tindall, Jonathan S.
Vandyke, Thomas J.
Vandyke, John H.
Vernon, Elijah.
Vernon, John T.
Vernon, Wm.
Wallace, Thomas J.
Welch, John M.
Wilkenson, James
Wycoff, John W.
Wycoff, James H.
Walker, Simon
Willis, James

Curtis, Francis
Duncan, James F.
Day, Hiram C.
Downing, George S.
Fort, Daniel
Feagins, Leonard B.
Forst, David
Foster, Joseph B.
Grant, John
Gregory, Enoch G.
Gregory, John W.
Gibson, Wm.
Gose, Stephen A.
Harding, John W.
McPheters, Jacob
McElroy, John J.
McKinney, Peter
Miner, Josiah
North, Layton H.
Nichols, Ozias D.
Nichols, John B.
Nichols, Joseph W.
Neal, Charles D. O.
Patterson, Hugh W.
Persons, George E.
Richardson, Nathaniel H.
Roan, Thomas T.
Roan, James M.
Walters, Peter
Walters, Wm. J.
Smith, James
Metcalf, James
Strait, Wm. B.
Wilson, Thomas M.
Millen, Robert A.
Jones, Thomas
Browning, Maxwell H.
Minor, Wm.
Ralston, David C.
Spurgeon, James H.
Booth, Jesse L.

COMPANY B.

JOHN P. YERGER, *Captain.*

WM. S. PARMELEY, *First Lieutenant.*

JOSEPH H. SHAWHAN, *Second Lieutenant.*

Alsup, John R.
Adams, David H.
Allen, John
Bratten, Andrew
Booton, George W.
Butler, Michael
Boegel, Henry H.
Boston, Asa S.
Basey James A.
Bell, Zephaniah
Bottger, John C.
Bradley, Samuel S.
Baxter, Lewis
Black, Philander
Basil, Jeremiah
Bowman, Henry V.
Crow, John H.
Clarahan, Michael J.
Clemmens, Henry
Connor, Aaron
Cole, Eleazer
Case, James H.
Carlile, Samuel
Courtney, James H.
Cattell, John W.
Fowler, David D,
Farmer, John L.
Ford, Jacob
Franklin, Joel
Givan, Henry C.
Gann, Leander O.
Gann, John L.
Griffin, Harlan
Harter, Joseph J.
Howard, John W.
Harris, William
Hax, John
Herrell, James B.
Hardesty, Samuel B.
Jacobs, James B.
Jenner, Thomas A.
Jones, Wm. H.
Keener, John W. C.
Kensler, George
Klett, Godfrey,
Lambert, David
Lee, John
Lowe, James M.
Landers, Henry J.
Leonard, Francis M.
Malone, James H.
Newkirk, Jacob H.
Nichols, John E.
Nelson, William D.
Nelson, William H.
O'Niel, John S.
Payton, George, jr,
Payton, John
Payton, William,
Payton, George,
Quick, Tennis
Quick, Stheter
Quick, James
Randall, Machron W.
Randall, Charles,
Rogers, Hannibal
Shawhan, George W.
Smith, Zelek C.
Shallenberger, Hiram
Stout, George W.
Thompson, Albert J.
Thompson, Thomas J.
Thompson, Albert E,
Trueblood, Elijah,
Utterback, Jefferson

Case, John H.
Clarahan, Patrick
Case, George C.
Crooks, Jacob V.
Courtney, Howard F.
Carson, Henry S.
Chrisman, John
Davis, James H.
Duree, George W.
Duree, Henry F.
Decker, Dennis
Dyer, Francis M.
Evans, Samuel B.
Evans, Gideon L.
Eastburn, John B.
Fear, James H.
Long, George W.
Matthews, Fenelon B.
Myers, Thomas B.
Mead, Augustus M.
Miles, John
McCalley, Jacob
Miles, Daniel
Moore, Robert
McGonegal, Charles
Moore, Joseph C.
Menefee, John
Morgan, Nathan
McGrew, Leander
Miller, Jacob E.
McAdams, Edwin J.
Malin, Wm.
Wescott, Benjamin
Wright, William A.
Wilson, David
Ward, William F.
Ward, Samuel A.
Woolard, James F.
Wertz, Francis M.
Wait, Reuben
Stout, Wm. H.
Moffat, Wm. A.
Long, Edward.
Henderson, Wm.
Tucker, Leander.
Cark, Wm. B.

COMPANY C.

ANDREW J. COMSTOCK, *Captain.*
ROBERT F. BURTON, *First Lieutenant.*
CYRUS H. TALBOT, *Second Lieutenant.*

Armstrong, David
Adair, James
Adair, Marion
Butler, Frederick
Barlean, Samuel
Barlean, Jonas
Butler, Jacob B.
Baker, James W.
Baldwin, Sylvester
Bartlett, Owen P.
Berry, James M.
Currey, George G.
Coomes, Reuben
Crowder, Thomas
Crowder, Charles
Chick, Elijah J.
Castleman, Amanuel
Coomes, Henry
Chick, James E.
Coterell, Wesley
Crayton, James
Campbell, Wm.
Currier, Edward
Goodwin, James H. D.
Graham, Sandford
Garey, Frederick
Grant, Cyrus A.
Grace, James R.
Grace, John R.
Gooden, Thomas G.
Graham, Edward
Groves, John H.
Goodwin, Abraham
Graham, Nelson
Hook, Norman R.
Harper, Joseph
Harris, Wm. H.
Harris, Wm.
Holton, Richard W.
Johnston, Oliver
Joy, Solomon
Jones, Alonzo
Jackson, Mortimer
Jones, Wm. R.
Kissick, Robert
Kindig, Allen R.
Myers, Wm. F.
Nation, James F.
Osborn, Wm.
Pilgrim, John R.
Patten, Wm. H.
Petty, Amos D.
Patten, John M.
Rardin, Jethro
Ryan, Jacob S.
Reaves, James H.
Ryan, Samuel
Scott, James B.
Stroud, Wm. H.
Sharp, George H.
Spain, James B.
Stephens, George W.
Stewart, Joseph P.
Spain, Joshua
Schee, George W.
Talbott, Robert
Talbott, Richard J.
Timbrel, Lot
Vancleve, Samuel G.

Curry, Robert W. B.
Chaplain, James M.
Duke, Hamilton
Davis, George R.
Delong, Thomas E.
Dove, George W.
Dove, John
Dodge, Wm.
Eckroate, John
Ellis, Wm. A.
Ellington, Michael W.
Ellington, John D.
Foreman, George
Fox, Joab
Fenn, Deno
Gaunt, John F.
Kindig, Oliver J.
Kunzman, John George
Kirkpatrick, James W.
Knight, Samuel
Keeser, Rezin
Lundy, Wm.
Lundy, George W.
Ladington, Henry C.
Lincoln, Levi W.
Leatherman, John S.
Mills, Elias
McBride, Harvey C.
Morrow, Wm. W.
Mullen, Isaac A.
McIntosh, Wm.
McIntosh, Jeremiah
Victor, Wm.
Vancleve, Albert
Wells, Joshua B.
Wilson, Wm.
Wilson, Clark
Wilson, Robert
Wright, Joshua
Weense, John
Winn, Robert
Walker, Wm. B.
Williams, John B.
Yeadon, Samuel
Sharp, George
Wright, John
Ream, John T.

COMPANY D.

JOHN LOFLAND, *Captain.*

DENNY M. GUNN, *First Lieutenant.*

RILEY JESSUP, *Second Lieutenant.*

Adams, George
Atwood, Moses F.
Adams, David
Appleton, Clark
Atwood, Stephen
Bennett, Charles G.
Brower, David M. C.
Bass, Andrew J.
Berkey, Albert G.
Brewster, Philander
Batterson, Edwin B.
Brundedge, Levi E.
Boyer, Wm. E.
Brown, Nathaniel H.
Burris, Stacey
Bupp, Frank
Blackstone, Thomas J.
Crawford, John R.
Counsel, Oran
Champ, Thornton
Coe, Alven H.
Cope, Henry
Collins, John C.
Hines, Ezra F.
Houser, Jacob
Hughes, Jared
Hilliard, William
Hopkins, Abraham C.
Hiner, Jesse
Hiner, David
Hiner, Wm.
Hiatt, Amos
Hull, Benjamin
Heaverlo, Andrew
Hewson, Samuel
Hull, Ahalial
Jones, John W.
Kindig, Wm. H.
Killough, John H.
Kirkpatrick, George N.
Leighton, Henry C.
Locke, Wm. G.
Lacey, John F.
Likens, Wm.
Lafollett, John W.
Larkins, J. W.
Reeder, Pemberton
Rockwell, Alanson
Reams, Vincent
Randall, Jefferson
Stephens, David
Slater, Elisha W.
Roberts, James M.
Rice, Eugene W.
Schwalm, Albert W.
Stevens, Hugh
Sandiland, Wm. A.
Sandiland, Alexander
Shannon, John A.
Stout, Thomas C.
Shelley, Benjamin F.
Smith, Wm. F.
Tracy, Wm.
Tracy, Marion
Totman, Nathaniel
Thompson, Joseph
Talbot, Wm. H.
Trobridge, Wm.
Thompson, David R.

Clark, Henry M.
Darrow, James E.
Doughman, Samuel H.
Doughman, Andrew J.
Deweese, Wm. J.
Deweese, Samuel L.
Deweese, John B.
Donelson, Amos W.
Dixon, Harvey M.
Dilley, David M.
Ewing, John N.
Ellis, Adelbert L.
Evans, Wm. L.
Enos, Wm.
Fagan, Wm.
Flanders, Nathan N.
Garden, Thomas J.
Grey, Amos
Moore, Eliphaz
Middleton, Jesse H.
Mahaffey, John
McKinsey, David P.
Michener, Henry P.
McNeal, Henry P.
Mitchell, George R.
Needham, David L.
Newton, Henry
Pope, Washington C.
Peckover, Wm.
Peters, Wm. C.
Proctor, Jefferson,
Proctor, Wm.
Packer, Isaac W. D.
Peckover, John
Quaintance, Morris A.
Ramey, John H.
Vickers, Sandford
Vickroy, Lewis F.
Williams, Thomas J.
Winder, Hugh W.
Widows, James H.
Wood, David J. M.
Warner, James M.
Williams, John D.
White, Wm. L.
Windsor, Joseph
West, Isaac W.
Young, John C.
Zane, Wm. L.
Thorp, Wm.
Mendenhall, Wm.
Barr, Pinckney F.

COMPANY E.

JOHN P. WALKER, *Captain.*
CHENEY PROUTY, *First Lieutenant.*
T. L. SEEVERS, *Second Lieutenant.*

Allen, Elam
Armel, William
Breckenridge, John A.
Blackstone, Wm. M.
Boyer, Richard M.
Brown, Hale B. W.
Brown, John D.
Bones, John
Baughman, Elias
Barnes, William A.
Boswell, Joshua R.
Brittain, James F.
Bird, Willis S.
Bowers, Wm. J.
Burket, Magnus D.
Beal, Nicholas
Bacon, Daniel
Cochran, Lewis H.
Crewder, Robert S.
Cratty, Wm. M.
Capper, Howard
Glendenning, James E.
Gosnell, Samuel D.
Gosnell, Jesse S.
Grover, James W.
Hines, George
Haleman, James W.
Harris, John B.
Harris, Wm. B.
Howard, Walter
Hawk, Anthony
Hawk, Wm. W.
Himes, Jacob M.
Holloway, John S.
Haney, Jacob D.
Harland, Humphrey M.
Horn, John W.
Haydock, Daniel W.
Hinckle, Thomas H.
Hall, Zachariah T.
Himes, Theodore
Haynes, Robert H.
Ruby, Tilford H.
Roland, George
Ruby, Martin C.
Ross, Wm. A.
Robb, George L.
Reno, Wm. C.
Robertson, Samuel S.
Robertson, William A.
Redpath, Joseph
Redpath, James A.
Snoak, Henry
Sawyer, James H.
Shaver, Levi C.
Shaw, Levi
Shaw, Charles W.
Satchell, James W.
Shelledy, Leander K.
Stoltzer, Stephen
Sumner, Wm. H.
Smith, Marion D.
Stephenson, Charles M.

Clammer David
Church, Alonzo M.
Corns, Amos
Cochran, John D.
Cruzen, Benjamin
Church, Washington
Carson, George S.
Chadwick, Wheeler
Dunbar, Marion
Davis, Clement A.
Dodd, Charles J.
Downing, Wm. H.
Eveland, Linas J.
Eveland, Frank
Eichelbarger, Adam
Finney, John M.
Faucett, George
Glenn, Wm. S.
Haleman, Alexander M.
Kinsman, Theodore S.
Kirkendall, Joseph W.
Lockhart, Isaac M.
Lyster, Asher W.
Miller, Henry T.
McMullen, Philander
McCully, Wm. S.
McLean, John
McLean, Alexander
McCullough, James
Miller, John H.
Nolan, Eugene
Ogden, James
Plumley, James S.
Phillips, John
Perrigo, Ambrose
Redpath, James T.
Slamel, Peter
Tipton, Joshua D.
Whitaker, John
West, John
Wharton, John S.
Wilson, David G.
Whitaker, Reuben
Wells, John W.
Welch, Hiram
Wilson, Abel F.
Williams, Joseph
Young, Jonathan E.
Young, Thomas H.
Kitsmiller, Norman B.
Green, William L.
Likes, Robert B.

COMPANY F.

MEMORIAL W. FORREST, *Captain.*
ANDERSON DAVIS, *First Lieutenant.*
LYCURGUS McCOY, *Second Lieutenant.*

Allison, Wm.
Abrams, Wm.
Abrams, Miles
Allen, Westley
Allison, Thomas J.
Abrams, James
Armstrong, James H.
Bell, James W.
Bell, John
Botkin, Zebedee T.
Braden, Robert C.
Baxter, George F.
Belvel, Samuel
Buckner, Ashley A.
Belvel, Nicholas
Brunt, John M.
Britain, Eli
Britain, Harvey
Bly, James H.
Cushman, Orland D.
Dickerson, James C.
Hart, John S.
Hutton, James K. P.
Hoisington, Wm. V.
Hadley, Joseph H.
Hobson, Joel
Hugh, James A.
Hone, John C.
Hemingher, Henry S.
Hawk, Cornelius
Hagan, Charles M.
Hough, Wm. P.
Hadley, Sidney C.
Hughes, George H.
Jones, John M.
Kawk, Jacob S.
Loomis, Nelson
Lotspeech, Samuel P.
Lynch, Paul A.
Logan, Henry
Larimore, John
McCreary, John
Mitchell, Wm. W.
Morgan, John B.
McCreary, James
Nugent, John F.
Nash, Charles W.
Nash, Asa B.
Orndorff, Wm.
Pratt, George A.
Robinson, Wm. S.
Rayburn, John C.
Sechrist, Abraham
Spears, James R.
Sanchezteresо, Frederick
Shepherd, Samuel
Street, Samuel F.
Sheets, Leander
Stillwell, Thomas
Spears, Ezra T.
Stillwell, George F.
Skinner, Jasper
Stillwell, George W.

Day, Valentine
Durfey, Orson M.
Day, Charles R.
Day, Abraham
Furgerson, James T.
Furgerson, Russell
Gaston, Wm. J.
Gill, James
Graves, Johnson
Groesbeck, George W.
Glass, Alexander W.
Gibson, Francis M.
Gibson, Walker B.
Golliher, Charles B.
Hillery, Milton

Monohan, Wm.
McPherson, John
Mills, Eli
Miller, Eli
McNies, Wm.
Montgomery, Samuel B.
McConnel, Wm. J.
Monohon, David
Minor, John N.
McConnel, Francis M.
McCreary, Daniel
McNies, John
McNies, Pleasant
Morrison, James
Miller, Joseph T.

Smith, Marion
Thomas, Gideon
Trent, John
Trent, Josiah
Waugh, Albert F.
Walker, Edwin
Ward, Wm.
Wood, Christopher
Young, James M.
Brenette, George S.
Stewart, Jacob F.
Miller, Asa M.
Miller, John W.
Bennett, Sanford G.
Schank, John Jacob

COMPANY G.

LAURISTON W. WHIPPLE, *Captain.*

GEORGE R. LEDYARD, *First Lieutenant.*

JOHN C. KLIJN, *Second Lieutenant.*

Aikins, Henry D.
Baldwin, Samuel A.
Bauman, Hendrick
Beard, Wm. E.
Black, Jonathan M.
Bowman, Jacob L.
Bousquet, Henry L.
Bruijn, Kryn de
Blockland, Tunis
Cory, Lewis P.
Cox, Thomas W.
Clark, William D.
Canine, Cornelius
Croll, Daniel W.
Campbell, William P.
Davenport, James H.
Dingeman, John W.
Dingeman, Daniel
Downing, William H. H.
Dunaway, Thomas B.
Dungan, Joseph W.
Dunnick, Cornelius
Downs, Wm. O.
Dunnington, Orville R.

Haven, John Q.
Kock, Stephanus de
Klyne, Cornelius
Lemmons, Jacob
Morgan, John S.
Miller, Jacob
McMichael, David
Metz, John
McCollum, Andrew J.
McCullough, Wm. S.
McLeod, John
Mathes, Valentine
Martin, Larkin
Myers, Holland
Moore, Nathan O.
Moore, Alexander
Martin, Levi
Myers, Delano
Niermeyer, John
Nelson, Frank
Niermyer, John, jr.
Owen, John W.
Pruit, Francis M.
Prouty, Flavius A.

Steenwyk, Gerard Van
Steenwyk, John G. Van
Smith, James S.
Smiley, Wm. P.
Sipna, Sjoerd R.
Shull, Richard P.
Shull, Jacob H.
Shull, Charles M.
Steadman, Benjamin T
Stearman, Robert H.
Templeton, Amaziah
Towne, George W.
Tol, Deik,
Thomas, Wm. H.
Thomas, Theodore F.
Taylor, Jacob
Ulsh, Henry J.
Ulsh, Daniel G.
Vanness, Daniel
Versteig, Gyskrt
Vanderkamp, Gerrit
Vandermœlen, Sijtz S. S.
Vandermeer, Isaac [R. P.
Vandermaa, Henry J.

Englesma, Martin
Earp, Wm. H.
Fidler, John K.
Ford, James H.
Fisk, Harvey
Griffith, Wm. V.
Garrison, John
Green, John
Herbert, Henry C.
Henry, John
Hansell, Samuel
Hol, Martinus
Haze, Peter J.
Hamrick, Allen
Hamilton, Wm. H.
Hamilton, Joseph D.
Price, Gilmore
Peters, Julius A. M.
Perkins, Ezra H.
Ritner, Isaac N.
Reynolds, Lucien
Rubertus, Herman D.
Roberts, James P.
Richardson, George R.
Rhynsburger, John J.
Robbins, Charles H.
Sharman, Charles H.
Sleyster, Warnerus
Schippers, Nicholas
Sperry, Andrew F.
Squires, John
Stallard, Luke
Vorhies, Sanford
Vineyard, Thomas
Veenschoten, Evert Van
Vorhies, Wm.
Wheeler, Harman
Woods, Enos M.
Wallace, Thomas D.
Wiser, Daniel
Williamson, Thomas
Watkins, Joseph F.
Walraven, Martin
Ward, Benjamin F.
White, Thomas J.
Wycoff, John W.
Zeenu, Cornelius de

COMPANY H.

JOHN DILLON, *Captain.*
JOSEPH L. SMITH, *First Lieutenant.*
WILLIAM GORE, *Second Lieutenant.*

Adams, Wilson
Allen, William
Ashley, George
Beardsley, Robert B.
Bales, Levi M.
Brown, Stephen J.
Boon, Clark
Brumback, Garrison
Brunson, William D.
Brunson, Newton H.
Cooper, Albert
Campbell, Lewis
Cunningham, John B.
Curby, Abram R.
Cabler, Daniel
Cline, Jacob
Curby, Jeremiah
Campbell, Joseph
Campbell, Wesley
Clark, Thomas J
Campton, James D.
Campbell, Samuel
Coffman, James A.
Gow, Daniel A.
Gow, Jefferson
Holland, David O.
Hollingsworth, Ezra
Hayworth, James D.
Holliday, Jerome
Holloway, David
Hermon, James
Heald, Henry
Hardenhook, John
Herr, William
Hoyt, William R.
Hall, Reuben M.
Hildebrand, Samuel M.
Irwin, William
Irons, Charles
Irons, John
Johnson, Frank
Linebarger, Samuel
Lawler, Thomas J.
Lane, John T.
Landreth, Harvey
Landry, Thomas
Riley, Joseph H.
Roland, Joseph M.
Rodman, William M.
Suitor, Joseph L.
Simms, Ellington T.
Stephenson, Thomas
Simpson, Thomas
Shanafelt, John W.
Suitor, Philip
Schoville, William
Smith, John V
Shanafelt, Owen K.
Smith, William H.
Stokesbury, James H.
Sanders, Samuel R.
Swails, Jacob
Seaton, Oliver
Slate, Lorenzo
Shanafelt, George W.
Shoff, John
Smith, Aaron B.
Smith, Philip S.
Turner, Henry J.

Currier, Victor
De Garmo, Wilson
Disor, John W.
Dison, William T.
Doty, Ezra
Dorman, Hiner
Decker, Elisha
Decker, Francis M.
Eaton, John C.
Edmondson, William F.
Eaton, Marcus D.
Ford, Usarius C.
Fry, John
Fry, David
Fish, William J.
Franken, Bartholomew
Garrett, James
Goldthwait, Charles J.
Lakin, Thomas
Lakin, John W.
Marling, George W.
McCombs, Benjamin M.
Mills, Elwood
McCord, Alfred J.
McNiel, Allen A.
McNeal, Owen P.
Moore, William J.
Nathlich, Adelbert
Nelson, Edward
Nyswanner, David
Newport, Jesse
Peck, Marion A.
Paul, Charles M.
Potts, Sedwick
Parks, William J.
Peterson, Augustus
Tracy, Hezekiah W.
Thomas, Milton
Tate, Martin V.
Thompson, Lloyd P.
Thompson, Thomas M.
Ward, Samuel C.
Wightman, John
Wandling, Jacob
Ward, John
Waltze, Benjamin F.
Withrell, Chauncey
Wright, James H.
Wells, Bloomfield E.
Wandling, Jacob A.
Wilson, James M.
Balls, James H.

COMPANY I.

PARIS T. TOTTEN, *Captain.*

JOHN HENDERSON, *First Lieutenant.*

JOHN REICHARD, *Second Lieutenant.*

Allison, John D.
Applegate, George W.
Anderson, John H.
Brobst, Josiah
Brobst, Joseph
Banta, Smith
Bawman, Sylvanus
Bonebrake, Peter A.
Bruett, John
Clark, Joseph M.
Carrothers, Levi
Coura, William P.
Conwell, George
Carder, Henry
Carrothers, William J.
Dennis, Azariah
Dunlap, Smith
De Witt, Henry J.
Fisher, Joseph
Furgerson, Hans
Funk, William P.
Hutchinson, Daniel
Henderson, John M.
Haynes, Clayton T.
Hutchinson, Arnold C.
Hays, James M.
Hornback, Jacob
Horn, Levi P.
Henry, John
Harman, Peter
Henderson, William M.
Hart, James H.
Houghar, George
Irons, William
Jones, Oscar L.
Jacobs, Hubbard
Layton, John
Lemburger, Frederick
Limes, Edgar F.
Long, John W.
McCorkel, John Y.
Mears, John W.
Penland, Evan B.
Reed, Preston A.
Richards, Josiah
Ream, Walter
Ridgewav, John H.
Rowland, William
Rankin, Andrew M.
Rankin, Harvey
Riddel, Joseph
Reed, William G.
Strong, Samuel L.
Stephens, Drury S.
Smith, David S.
Smith, George J.
Smith, Thomas
Scott, Alexander
Stanfield, George W.
Strong, James W.
Spohn, Hezekiah
Shepherd, John N.
Snyder, John S.

Funk, Isaac N.
Farlee, Henry
Gibson, Alpheus W.
Gunter, Henry B.
Gafford, James A.
Godfrey, Thaddeus
Graham, William H.
Goff, William
Goodwin, Nathan D.
Graham, William
Goodenough, Eri
Gaston, James A.
Gaston, Ephraim C.
Gibson, Jacob B.
Hessenflow, John S.
Hessenflow, John F.
McMillen, Samuel
Manor, Samuel
McCorkel, Joseph L.
McCleland John M.
Maddy, John W.
McCorkel, John W.
McMillen, Henry
McMillen, Alexander
Newman, James A.
Neal, Solon S.
Parker, William H.
Palmer, Enoch
Pitts, Joseph P.
Pope, William W.
Pearson, Ira A.
Pearson, Young
Spohn, John
Schee, James
Teed, George R.
Templin, John
Terry, Dennis
Vandlah, John S.
Willey, Nathaniel D. T.
Willey, Damon W.
Wolf, William W.
Wolf James M.
Walsh, James J.
Welch, David T.
Woodward, Jacob
Woodward, Calvin
Welcher, Andrew

COMPANY K.

THORNTON McINTOSH, *Captain.*
GEORGE GILCHRIST, *First Lieutenant.*
JOHN M. BAUGH, *Second Lieutenant.*

Andrews, Thomas R.
Ashmead, James T.
Agnew, James
Allgood, Jefferson
Anderson, William H.
Boswell, John
Blair, Robert
Bell, James M.
Boyd, William
Broyles, Samuel
Buntain, Cary A.
Burgess, Amos
Burgess, Andrew J.
Boyd, Robert F.
Boswell, Levi
Burgess, James S.
Burgess, John
Connor, Thomas R.
Crozier, Thomas S.
Cowan, William R.
Collins, Merrill P.
Crozier, Matthew W.
Carnahan, Francis
Gilchrist, Matthew D.
Gordon, Jasper H.
Gaston, Cyrus
Gregory, William
Gaston, David
George, Jacob
Heath, Harvey S.
Haskell, Royal
Huff, Charles A.
Higgins, Thomas
Haskell, Daniel
Haskell, Henry C.
Hartman, Robert R.
Howell, William H.
Harris, Augustus A.
Henry, John N.
Henderson, Enoch F.
Hornback, James B.
Jones, Alexander
Jackson, William M.
Kernahan, Thomas A,
Kunnen, Francis
Loughridge, James
Moore, William H.
Nichol, David F.
Porter, John
Playle, Francis M.
Pettichord, Wm, H. H.
Padget, James
Rankin, William A.
Robertson, Darius
Robinson, James
Rea, John B.
Rea, Cyrus
Roberts, John C.
Remington, Sylvester
Ryan, Charles E.
Reed, Andrew R.
Shaw, William H.
Stratton, George B.
Smith, Franklin
Shipley, James B.
Stephenson, James M.
Smith, Samuel H.
Smith, Ephraim S.
Tucker, Leander O.

Criss, John
Correll, Carey A.
Coleburn, William H.
Drinkle, Henry S.
Dysart, David
Dixon, Matthew
Douglas, John W.
Dixon, Nathan C.
Eastburn, Sanford
Evans, David T.
Emory, William T.
Elwell, Thomas
Foster, Benjamin
Fox, James B.
Furgerson, John
Loughridge, William
Lockard, Samuel L.
Musgrove, Benjamin H.
McAllister, William T.
Morgan, John G.
Miller, William G.
McFall, David
McKinney, William
McCune, David
Morgan, Lewis
Myers, David
Mershon, Felix G.
Morris, John A.
Martin, John W.
Myers, Jefferson
Todd, Benjamin
Tennis, Samuel M.
Williamson, Stephen A.
Williamson, Solomon
Walker, James A.
Wymore, Robert E.
Wagoner, Lazarus
Williamson, Alburn M.
Withrow, William H.
Windell, James
Wymore, Jasper H.
Jackson, Hugh M.
Jackson, James M.

PROMOTIONS, ETC.

PROMOTIONS, ETC.

The following are the more important changes by promotion, &c., in the companies, as far as can be given from present data:

COMPANY A.

Captain C. B. Boydston, promoted to Major, June 29th, 1864.
Second Lieutenant E. K. Woodruff, resigned, March 3d, 1863.
First Sergeant James M. Cooper, promoted to Second Lieutenant, April 12th, 1863; and to First Lieutenant, July 21st, 1864.
First Sergeant A. W. Bishop, promoted to Second Lieutenant, Dec. 11th, 1864.
First Lieutenant S. S. Pierce, promoted to Captain.

COMPANY B.

Captain John P. Yerger, resigned, May 10th, 1864.
First Lieutenant Joseph H. Shawhan, resigned, March 25th, 1863.
Second Lieutenant Wm. S. Parmeley, promoted to First Lieutenant, May 20th, 1863; and to Captain, June 7th, 1864.
Second Sergeant Joseph J. Harter, promoted to Second Lieutenant, July 1st, 1863; and to First Lieutenant, June 7th, 1864.

COMPANY C.

First Lieutenant Robert F. Burton, resigned, April 8th, 1863.
Second Lieutenant Cyrus H. Talbott, resigned, June 2d, 1863.
Fourth Sergeant Oliver J. Kindig, promoted to Second Lieutenant, Oct. 16th, 1863.
First Sergeant Joshua B. Wells, promoted to First Lieutenant, Sept. 22d, 1864 and to Captain Dec. 8th, 1864.
Second Sergeant Robert Kissick, promoted to Adjutant of 113th A. D., March March 28th, 1864.
Sergeant Norman R. Hook, promoted to Second Lieutenant, Jan. 7th, 1865.

COMPANY D.

Captain John Lofland, promoted to Lieutenant-Colonel, April 23d, 1864.
First Lieutenant Denny M. Gunn, resigned, Oct. 24th, 1864.
Second Lieutenant Riley Jessup, promoted to Captain, May 24th, 1864.
Second Sergeant Henry C. Leighton, promoted to Second Lieutenant, July 21st, 1864; and to First Lieutenant Dec. 22d, 1864.
Private D. J. Woods, promoted to Adjutant of 14th Kansas Cavalry, March, 1863.

Second Sergeant John R. Crawford, promoted to Sergeant-Major, April 16th, 1863.

Fourth Sergeant Charles G. Bennett, promoted to Quarter-Master Sergeant, April 10th, 1864.

Albert G. Berkey, promoted to Commissary Sergeant in 1864.

Amos Hiatt, promoted to Second Lieutenant, Dec. 22d, 1864.

COMPANY E.

Captain John P. Walker, resigned, April 2d, 1863.

First Lieutenant Cheney Prouty, promoted to Captain, May 10th, 1863.

Second Lieutenant T. L. Seevers, promoted to First Lieutenant, May 10th, 1863.

Second Sergeant John A. Breckinridge, promoted to Second Lieutenant, June 2d, 1863; resigned May 26th, 1864.

Private Reuben Whitaker, promoted to Hospital Steward, April 22d, 1864.

Private David Clammer, promoted to Captain in 54th A. D., Aug. 26th, 1863.

Private George Fawcett, promoted to Second Lieutenant in 54th A. D., Sept. 3d, 1863.

COMPANY F.

Captain M. W. Forrest, resigned, March 13th, 1863.

First Lieutenant Anderson Davis, resigned, April 24th, 1863.

Second Lieutenant Lycurgus McCoy, resigned, March 13th, 1863.

Corporal John Bell, promoted to Captain, April 16th, 1863.

Second Sergeant Frederick Sancheztereso, promoted to First Lieutenant, June 2d, 1863.

First Sergeant William J. Gaston, promoted to Second Lieutenant, March 14th, 1863; resigned Oct., 25th, 1863.

Private Abraham Sechrist, promoted to Second Lieutenant in 54th A. D., Aug. 26th, 1863.

COMPANY G.

Captain Lauriston W. Whipple, promoted to Lieutenant-Colonel of 113th A. D., June 18th, 1864.

First Lieutenant George R. Ledyard, promoted to Captain, July 21st, 1864.

Second Lieutenant John C. Klijn, resigned, February 24th, 1863.

Fifth Sergeant Charles H. Sharman, promoted to Second Lieutenant, March 1st, 1863, to First Lieutenant, July 1st, 1864, and to Adjutant, 186—.

First Sergeant Lewis P. Cory, promoted to Second Lieutenant, July 21st, 1864, and to First Lieutenant, ——.

First Sergeant Wm. V. Griffith, promoted to Captain in 113th A. D., May 26th, 1864.

First Sergeant John S. Morgan, promoted to Second Lieutenant, February 21st, 1865.

A. F. Sperry, promoted to Principal Musician, May 1st, 1863.

COMPANY H.

Captain John Dillon, resigned, July 26th, 1863.

First Lieutenant Joseph L. Smith, resigned, April 8th, 1863.

Second Lieutenant William H. Gore, promoted to First Lieutenant, April 9th, 1863, and to Captain, January 1st, 1864.

First Sergeant Wilson DeGarmo, promoted to Second Lieutenant, April 9th, 1863, and to First Lieutenant, July 27th, 1864.

First Sergeant David A. Holland, promoted to Second Lieutenant, April 22d, 1864.

COMPANY I.

Captain Paris T. Totten, died of wounds received at battle of Jenkin's Ferry, May 24th, 1864.

First Lieutenant John Henderson, resigned, March 25th, 1863.

Second Lieutenant John Reichard, promoted to First Lieutenant, March 26th, 1863; resigned, July 26th, 1863.

First Sergeant Joseph M. Clark, promoted to First Lieutenant, November 1st, 1863, resigned, March 30th, 1864.

Second Sergeant Levi Carrothers, promoted to First Lieutenant, June 14th, 1864, and to Captain, July 21st, 1864.

Third Sergeant Samuel L. Strong, promoted to Second Lieutenant, March 26th, 1863; resigned, May 20th, 1864.

Sergeant Oscar L. Jones, promoted to First Lieutenant, July 21st, 1864.

First Sergeant Henry J. Gunter, promoted to Second Lieutenant in 113th A. D., May 27th, 1864.

COMPANY K.

Captain Thornton McIntosh, resigned, March 3d, 1863.

First Lieutenant George Gilchrist, resigned, March 3d, 1863.

Second Lieutenant John M. Baugh, promoted to Captain, March 4th, 1863; resigned, August 16th, 1864.

Fourth Sergeant Thomas R. Connor, promoted to First Lieutenant, March 4th, 1863; killed in battle of Jenkins' Ferry, April 30th, 1864.

Corporal Wm. A. Rankin, promoted to Second Lieutenant, March 4th, 1863, to 1st Lieutenant, July 21st, 1864, and to Captain, September 16th, 1864.

First Sergeant James Loughridge, promoted to First Lieutenant, September 16th, 1864.

Private Royal, promoted to Second Lieutenant in 54th A. D., July 26th, 1863.

Private Sanford Eastburn, promoted to First Lieutenant in 113th A. D., May 8th, 1864.

OFFICIAL REPORTS.

OFFICIAL REPORTS.

DEFENSE OF HELENA, ARKANSAS.

REPORT OF COLONEL S. A. RICE, COMMANDING BRIGADE.

HEAD-QUARTERS 2D BRIGADE, 13TH DIV., 13TH A. C., DEPT. OF THE TENN., HELENA, ARK., July 7th, A. D., 1863.

Captain A. Blocki, A. A. General,

CAPTAIN:—I have the honor to submit the following report of the part taken by the 2d Brigade in the action of the 4th inst.:

The 33d Missouri Infantry were stationed at Fort Curtis, and at Batteries A, B, C and D, which covered your entire line of defense. At all of these points they manned the artillery, and also had a reserve who acted as sharp-shooters.

The 33d Iowa Infantry was ordered to report to Fort Curtis, opposite the center of your line, at day-break, so that in case of an attack they might readily be thrown to the support of either wing, or the center of your line. At 4 o'clock, A. M., the enemy, in heavy force, drove in our pickets, and opened the engagement on Batteries A, C and D. The 33d Iowa was promptly, in compliance with your orders, moved into the rifle-pits, in front and flanking Batteries C and D, with a small portion acting as a reserve, who were posted so as to command the ravine between these batteries. Three companies of the 36th Iowa were sent at once to support Battery A and took possession of the rifle-pits flanking it. The 29th Iowa, with a reserve from the 36th, was ordered to take possession of the sides of the bluffs, on the east side, and a short distance in front of Battery A, extending down to the Sterling road, and drive the enemy from the crests of the hills which they already had occupied. On batteries C and D the main assault of the enemy was made. They hurled regiment after regiment, in closed column, against the works, but were gallantly repulsed at Battery D, and only after a severe and bloody conflict, took Battery C, driving our forces before them, but they promptly rallied, and formed at the bottom of the hill. The artillery from Batteries A, B and D, together with Fort Curtis, commanding Battery C, was opened upon the enemy, and after a severe cannonading, assisted by a galling fire from our infantry, they were driven back, with a heavy loss, and the battery retaken. The heavy loss sustained by the 33d Missouri and the 33d Iowa, on this portion of the field, fully attests their undoubted courage.

While the engagement was thus progressing in the center, the enemy were also concentrating a heavy fire on the right wing, which had been assigned to my command. They had planted a battery within four hundred yards of Battery A, but protected from its fire by a point of the hill; from the concentrated fire of the 1st Indiana Battery, (light artillery,) and a section of the 3d Iowa Battery, under Lieutenant Wright, assisted by our sharpshooters and a severe fire along the entire line, the enemy were compelled to withdraw their guns, with a severe loss. On this portion of our line the enemy had, besides their artillery, a brigade of four regiments of infantry, and a brigade of cavalry, under General Marmaduke, and at all points outnumbered us, at least four to one, according to their own estimates.

The officers and soldiers of the 29th Iowa acted with the utmost coolness and bravery, and steadily gained ground from the first onset. The 36th Iowa behaved in a manner worthy of all commendation. They were promptly moved to the relief of the 29th Iowa, and drove, by their well directed fire, the enemy before them, occupying the crests of the hills. The enemy could repeatedly be heard trying to rally their columns for the purpose of charging on our line, and were only prevented by the continuous fire of our line, assisted by a heavy and well directed cross fire from our artillery and the rifle-pits.

The 33d Missouri, manning the guns in the various batteries along the entire line, was at all points exposed to the hottest fire of the enemy, and deserve the highest praise for their bravery and efficiency. The heavy loss sustained by the enemy fully attests the bravery, the discipline, and efficiency of your entire command. There was taken by my command several hundred prisoners. We have buried one hundred and fifty-six of the enemy. There were also taken three stands of colors and several hundred stands of arms. The route of the enemy was complete at all points.

The loss in my command was forty-five killed, ninety-six wounded, and thirty missing. A full report of the above from each regiment, I append hereto. As a portion of my brigade, the 33d Iowa and part of the 33d Missouri, were in another part of the field from that assigned to my command, and acted more immediately under your own observation, I trust, in case I have not been able to present fully the part they took in the action, that you will supply the deficiency in your official report. A detailed account of the part taken by the various regiments of the brigade, would involve not only what was done by them but by other brigades, who bore an equally honorable part in the entire engagement, and especially that of Colonel Clayton, of the 5th Kansas, who, with the 1st Indiana Battery and his cavalry, bore an important part in the engagement on the right of the line. When all did so well, invidious distinction would be out of place. If some bore more conspicuous parts than others, it was because the position of their own commands placed them in a more important position. I take especial pleasure in referring to Colonel Benton, of the 29th Iowa; Colonel Kittredge, of the 36th Iowa; Lieutenant-Colonel Heath, commanding 33d Missouri;

Lieutenant-Colonel Mackey, commanding 33d Iowa; Lieutenant-Colonel Patterson, 29th Iowa; Majors Gibson, Van Beck, and Shoemaker, who from their coolness, efficiency, and daring, are worthy of especial mention. They were at all times at the post of danger cheering their men. Lieutenant Lacy, my A. A. A. General, acted as my aid during the engagement, and rode to whatever part of the field required his presence, and afforded me assistance of the most valuable character, and I take especial pleasure in referring to him.

I am, Captain, very respectfully, your ob't serv't,

(Signed), SAMUEL A. RICE,

Colonel 33d Iowa Infantry, comd'g 2d Brigade.

CAPTURE OF LITTLE ROCK, ARKANSAS.

REPORT OF MAJOR-GENERAL STEELE.

HEAD-QUARTERS ARKANSAS EXPEDITION,
LITTLE ROCK, ARK., Sept. 12, 1863.

GENERAL:—I have the honor to submit the following as a summary of the operations which led to the occupation of the capital by the expeditionary army under my command.

On the 31st day of July I arrived at Helena, and pursuant to instructions from Major-General Grant, reported by letter to the commander of the 16th Army Corps for instructions relative to the fitting out of an expedition against Little Rock. General Hurlbut placed under my command all the troops at Helena, and the cavalry division under Brigadier-General Davidson, then operating in Arkansas. The garrison at Helena had been reinforced by two brigades of Kimball's division, which had just arrived from Snyder's Bluff, and were suffering severely from the malarious influences of the Yazoo country. The proportion of sick among the Helena troops was also very large. Three regiments were designated to remain at Helena, and these, with the sick and convalescents of the whole command were to constitute the garrison of that place. The troops at Helena designated for the expedition amounted to about six thousand (6,000) of all arms. There were three 6-gun and one 4-gun batteries, including six 10-pounder Parrott's. The cavalry, 1st Indiana, and 5th Kansas, amounted to less than (500) five hundred for duty. The 1st Indiana had three small rifled guns.

Davidson reported something less than (6,000) six thousand present for duty in his cavalry division, and (18) eighteen pieces of artillery—showing an aggregate of about (12,000) twelve thousand for duty. Brigadier-Generals Kimball and Salomon obtained leave of absence, and the resignation of General Ross was accepted, which left me with but one general officer, Davidson

The resignation of my A. A. General was accepted just at this time, and there were no officers of the quartermaster or subsistence department at Helena, except Captain Allen, A. C. S., and Captain Noble, A. Q. M., who were in charge of the stores in the depot. I ordered the establishment of camps for the sick and convalescents, and organized the command in the best manner possible. Davidson pushed on to Clarendon and established a ferry for crossing troops, corduroying two miles of bottom and laying down the pontoon bridges across the Rock Rae bayou. On the 10th of August the Helena troops, organized into a division under Colonel, now Brigadier-General, S. A. Rice, marched toward Clarendon, with orders to reconstruct the bridges which had been destroyed by the rebels and to make all necessary repairs on the road, which was in bad condition.

Kimball's division, under Colonel McLean, followed next day. The whole command was at Clarendon and commenced crossing the river on the 17th of August. Before the crossing was effected I found my operations encumbered by over (1,000) one thousand sick. To have established a hospital and depot at this point would have involved the necessity of occupying both sides of the river. Duvall's Bluff was a more healthy location, and the route from there to Little Rock possessed many advantages over the other as a line of operations. I therefore ordered all the stores and sick to be sent to Duvall's Bluff by water. The enemy had constructed rifle-pits in a commanding position fronting the crossing on Rock Rae bayou, but, on the approach of Davidson's division, had fallen back, leaving only a picket. This position could easily have been turned by the road leading up from Harris's ferry.

On the 22d Davidson was directed to move with his division to Deadman's lake and reconnoiter the enemy's position at Brownsville. On the 23d the rest of the command moved to Duvall's Bluff, the transports carrying the sick and stores under convoy of the gun-boats. An advantageous site was selected on the bluff for a hospital and depot, and details immediately ordered to throw up intrenchments, cut away the timber on the flanks to give the gun-boats clear view and range, to erect sheds, &c.

On the 24th Davidson advanced to Two Prairie bayou, and on the 25th continued the march, skirmishing with Marmaduke's cavalry up to Brownsville, dislodging him at that place, and driving him into his intrenchments at bayou Metoe on the 20th. The attack was renewed on the 27th, and the enemy driven from his works on the bayou, and fired the bridge as he retreated. Davidson was unable to save the bridge, everything having been prepared for the destruction before hand. The bayou was deep and miry, and the pursuit of the rebels being thus checked, Davidson withdrew to his camp at Brownsville, leaving pickets at the crossings on the bayou. I received information that True's brigade from Memphis would arrive at Clarendon on the 20th, and immediately sent a party to construct a bridge across Rock Rae bayou, and a ferry-boat to cross the troops over White river. True crossed on the 30th of August, and on the 1st of September moved up to Deadman's lake. The advance from Duvall's Bluff also commenced on the 1st, the place having been put in such a state of defense that the convalescents and a small detail left there were deemed sufficient to hold it against any force the enemy would be likely to send against it. On the 2d instant all my available force was concentrated at Brownsville. It had been ascertained that the military road on the south side of Bayou Metoe passed through a section impracticable for any military operations—swamp, timber, and entanglements of vines and undergrowth, and was commanded by the enemy's works. I therefore directed Davidson to make a reconnoissance in force around the enemy's left by way of Austin, and, if practicable, to penetrate his lines and ascertain both his strength and position. Rice's division was ordered forward to make a diversion in Davidson's favor on Bayou Metoe. Rice drove in the enemy's pickets, shelled the woods on the south side of the bayou for several hours, and encamped for the night. In the meantime, Davidson pushed his reconnoissance until the numerous roads on his flanks and rear rendered it dangerous for him to proceed any further. The great length to which it would increase our line of communication with our base rendered it impracticable for us to attack the enemy on his left flank. This reconnoissance occupied two days.

By this time I had collected information in regard to the road leading by Shallow Ford and Ashley's Mills to the Arkansas and the right of the enemy's works, which determined me to take that route. The march to the front was resumed on the 6th. Here we found ourselves again encumbered with a large number of sick—near 700. True's brigade and Ritter's brigade of cavalry were left to guard the supply train and the sick. On the 7th we reached the Arkansas near Ashley's Mills. At this point, Davidson's cavalry, in advance, had a sharp skirmish with the enemy. The 8th and 9th were employed in reconnoissance, repairing the road back to Bayou Metoe, and in bringing up the sick and the supply train, with the two brigades left at Brownsville.

I had now definitely determined upon a plan of attack. Davidson was directed to lay the pontoon bridge at an eligible point, throw his division across the Arkansas river, and move directly on Little Rock, threatening the enemy's right flank and rear, while I moved with the rest of the force on the north flank and assailed the right of his works. During the night of the 9th Davidson made his dispositions for crossing the Arkansas, and on the morning of the 10th had the pontoon bridge laid. The second division was ordered to report to him at day-light to assist in covering his crossing. The bridge was placed in a bend of the river, and the ground on the south side was so completely swept by Davidson's artillery that the enemy could not plant a battery in any position from which he could interrupt the crossing.

Two regiments of infantry passed over the river to drive the enemy's skirmishers out of the woods, and the cavalry division passed on without serious interruption until they reached Bayou Fourche, where the enemy were drawn up in line to receive them. The rebels held their position obstinately until our artillery on the opposite side of the river was opened upon their flank and rear, when they gave way and were steadily pushed back by Davidson, the artillery constantly playing upon them from the other side of the river. Our two columns marched nearly abreast on either side of the Arkansas. Volumes of smoke in the direction of Little Rock indicated to us that the rebels had evacuated their works on the north side of the river, and were burning their pontoon bridges. Heavy clouds of dust moving down toward Davidson on the other side of the river made me apprehensive that the enemy contemplated falling upon him with his entire force. He was instructed in such an event to form on the beach, where his flanks could be protected by our artillery on the other side, and where aid might be sent to him by a ford. But they were in full retreat. Marmaduke's cavalry only were disputing Davidson's entry of the city. The rebels had fired three pontoon bridges laid across the Arkansas at the city, and several railroad cars. Two locomotives were also on fire, but were saved by us; part of the ponpoons were also saved. Six steamboats were entirely destroyed by fire, and we are informed that Price intended to have blown up the arsenal, but was pressed so close that he failed in this.

Our cavalry was too much exhausted to pursue the enemy's retreating columns far, on the evening of the 10th. Next morning Merrill's and Clayton's brigades renewed the chase and followed them twenty miles, taking a number of prisoners and causing the enemy to destroy a part of his train. Little Rock was formally surrendered by the municipal authorities on the evening of the 10th. Price had undoubtedly intended to give us battle in his intrenchments, but was entirely surprised by our movement across the Arkansas, and did not suspect it until after the pontoon bridge was laid. When it was reported to him that our infantry were crossing, he took it for granted that our whole force was moving to cut off his retreat to Arkadelphia. I have been assured by citizens that General Cabell, with about (4,000) four thousand troops from Fort Smith, had joined Price on his retreat, he having failed to reach here in time to assist in the defense of the place. I marched from Ashley's Mills on the morning of the 10th with not more than (7,000) seven thousand troops, having parked the trains and left a strong guard to defend them and the sick.

The operation of the army from the time that I commenced organizing it at Helena have occupied exactly forty days.

Our entire loss in killed, wounded, and prisoners, will not exceed (100) one hundred. The enemy's is much greater, especially in prisoners—at least (1,000) one thousand.

I shall reserve the list of casualties and my special recommendations for a future communication. However, I will say that Davidson and his cavalry division deserve the highest commendation.

I enclose Brigadier-General Davidson's report.

Very respectfully, your ob't serv't,

FRED. STEELE,

Major-General commanding.

Major-General SCHOFIELD, *Commanding Department of the Missouri.*

MARCH TO CAMDEN, ARKANSAS.

HEAD-QUARTERS 33D IOWA INFANTRY VOLUNTEERS,
CAMDEN, ARK., April 20, 1864.

John F. Lacy, A. A. A. General, 1st Brig., 3d Div., 7th Army Corps, and Army of Arkansas,

LIEUTENANT: In compliance with general orders from head-quarters 1st brigade, I herewith transmit you the following report pertaining to the 33d Regiment Iowa Infantry Volunteers, during the recent campaign, including lists of casualities, etc., etc.

Prior to the arrival of our forces at Prairie d'Anne, the part taken in any engagement by my regiment was entirely unimportant. On arriving at Prairie d'Anne, I was ordered to form line of battle and move to the left of the 50th Indiana, which was done. I was then ordered to form column by division, and in that order I moved forward on to the prairie. While crossing a slough in the timber joining the prairie, a shell from the enemy's gun exploded near the regiment, killing one man and breaking several guns. On reaching the open ground, I again deployed, sending forward two companies as skirmishers, with instructions to move steadily forward, which they did, driving the enemy before them, the regiment moving to their support. In this order I moved forward till the regiment rested where the enemy's artillery first opened fire. It then being dark, the skirmishers were ordered to rest in place, and the regiment retired two hundred yards to unexposed grounds, and bivouacked. At 11 o'clock P. M., the enemy dashed upon the skirmish line, but was repulsed without injury to us. The transactions of the following day are unimportant.

On the morning of the 13th of April, we moved, in connection with the entire forces, through and to the west of Prairie d'Anne, our skirmishers steadily driving the enemy before them. On approaching their works on the Camden and Washington road, the enemy hastily withdrew. From this time till the morning of the 15th, nothing worthy of note transpired.

On the 15th day of April, my regiment was the advance infantry. Two companies were deployed as skirmishers on either side of the road, and having moved forward two miles, were fired upon by the enemy. The skirmishers moved forward, driving them, assisted by a howitzer, until they came within range of the enemy's artillery, which was opened upon us, wounding four men. My regiment supported the 2d Missouri Battery on the right. Having taken this position, I sent forward three sharpshooters from each company to assist the skirmishers and annoy the enemy's gunners. After an engagement of two hours, the enemy withdrew from his position, after which the march was resumed. At about two miles distance, we were again fired on. While awaiting orders a shell from the enemy's gun burst near my regiment, dangerously wounding one man. A sharp skirmish was kept up for two and a half miles, when the enemy withdrew from our front.

Our entire loss in killed and wounded when we reached Camden amounted to one killed and four wounded.

I was relieved of my command on the 19th of April, while in camp at Camden, Colonel Mackey having arrived at the regiment.

H. D. GIBSON,
Major commanding regiment.

RETURN TO LITTLE ROCK.

HEAD-QUARTERS 33D IOWA INFANTRY VOLUNTEERS,
LITTLE ROCK, ARK., May 6th, 1864.

John F. Lacy, A. A. A. General, 1st Brig., 3d Div., 7th Army Corps,

LIEUTENANT: I have the honor herewith to transmit you the following report of the engagement in which the 33d Regiment Iowa Infantry took part from the time of my taking command at Camden, Ark., until its arrival at Little Rock, including a list of casualities, etc.

I arrived at Camden on the 19th day of April, and immediately took command of my regiment, at this time six hundred strong. Nothing of particular interest took place from the time of the evacuation of Camden until my arrival at Saline river. On the evening of the 29th, at 6½ o'clock P. M., I was ordered to the rear on the Camden road to support Colonel Inglemann's brigade, an attack being anticipated during the night. I stood at arms during the entire night, the enemy making no particular demonstration, although in speaking distance. Night very dark and raining most of the time.

About 4 o'clock A. M. on the 30th, I received orders that, as soon as the 43d Illinois Infantry on my left was withdrawn, I should retire about three-fourths of a mile towards the river, and take position covering the passage of the troops while crossing. This movement I executed without being discovered by the enemy. This position I occupied half an hour when the enemy made his appearance. The skirmishers immediately engaged them, holding them in check for half an hour. When I was relieved by the 27th Wisconsin Infantry, I marched my command to a new position, one mile in the direction of the crossing. In twenty minutes the engagement became general, and I was ordered to the support of the 50th Indiana Infantry on the left. From this time until the close of the battle, the regiment was almost continually engaged.

As to the conduct of both officers and men of my command, I can not speak in terms too high. To attempt distinction would be injustice to my command, as all did their duty nobly. A short time before the close of the action, I received a wound in my right arm, which compelled me to quit the field, the command of the regiment devolving upon Captain Boydston, Company A, who, at the close of the engagement, marched the regiment off in good order.

The regiment arrived in camp at Little Rock, Ark., on the 3d day of May, 1864. Nothing of importance transpired during the remainder of our march.

It would be doing great injustice to the enlisted men of my command to fail to notice the manner in which they endured the fatigue and privations of the march, the rations being exhausted on the 29th of April.

For the operations of the regiment prior to my command, reference is made to the report of Major H. D. Gibson, herewith transmitted.

With the highest respect,

Your obedient servant,

C. H. MACKEY, Colonel comd'g.

EXTENT OF CASUALTIES.

Killed—enlisted men, 8. Wounded—commissioned officers, 6; enlisted men, 96. Missing—enlisted men, 13. Total loss, 123.

CASUALTIES IN ARKANSAS.

List of Casualties in 33d regiment Iowa Infantry Volunteers, while in the field, from March 23d, 1864, to April 26th, 1864—Major H. D. Gibson, commanding.

KILLED.—William P. Funk, April 10th, struck in head by piece of shell.

WOUNDED, APRIL 15TH.—Enos M. Woods, leg, by piece of shell; Wm. H. Anderson, thigh, while skirmishing; John Burgess, leg, while skirmishing; William H. Withrow, hand, while skirmishing; all severely.

RECAPITULATION.—Total, killed, 1; wounded, 4; entire loss, 5.

List of Casualties in 33d regiment Iowa Infantry Volunteers, while in the field, from April 26th, 1864, to May 3d, 1864, time of the return of the command to Little Rock.

COMMISSIONED OFFICERS (ALL WOUNDED).—Colonel Cyrus H. Mackey, arm, severe; Captains A. J. Comstock, Co. C, thigh, severely, prisoner; Paris T. Totten, Co. I, thigh, severely, since died; 1st Lieuts. Thos. R. Conner, Co. K, neck, mortal, died in hands of enemy; Wilson DeGarmo, Co. H, hip, slight; 2d Lieut. Oliver I. Kindig, Co. C, leg, slight.

ENLISTED MEN, KILLED.—2d Sergt. John N. Ewing, Co. D, left on the field; Privates Thomas H. Hinkle, Co. E, left on the field; G. W. Shanafelt, Co. H, left on the field; J. M. Roland, Co. H, left on the field; Smith Banta, Co. I, left on the field; John M. Henderson, Co. I, left on the field; Sergt. Jasper Skinner, Co. F; Private Wm. A. Towbridge, Co. D.

WOUNDED.—Sergeant-Major John R. Crawford, thigh, severe, prisoner.

COMPANY A.—Corp'l John S. Johnston, leg, severe; Privates James T. Duncan, thigh, severe; Jonathan S. Tindall, hip, severe; Hiram P. Henry, thigh, severe; Alfred Hagar, shoulder, slight.

COMPANY B.—Dennis Decker, thigh, severe, prisoner; John E. Nichols, arm, severe; Francis M. Wertz, hand, slight.

COMPANY C.—1st Sergeant Joshua B. Wells, thigh, slight; Sergt. John T. Gaunt, shoulder, severe; Corp'l Reuben Coomes, arm, slight; Privates Mortimer Jackson, hip, slight, prisoner; John Dove, breast, severe, prisoner; Wm. B. Walker, thigh, slight, prisoner; Owen Bartlett, ankle, slight; Wm. Osborn, thigh, severe, prisoner; R. W. B. Curry, thigh, severe, prisoner; Edward Graham, groin, severe, prisoner.

COMPANY D.—Corp'ls John W. Jones, leg, severe, prisoner; Samuel Doughman, face, slight; Privates Samuel L. Deweese, arm, severe; Riley Mitchell, arm, severe, prisoner; David Adams, leg, severe, prisoner; Wm. Thorp, breast, severe, prisoner; Morris A. Quaintance, back, severe, prisoner.

COMPANY E.—2d Serg't John M. Finney, arm, slight; Corp'l David G. Wilson, shoulder, severe, prisoner; Privates Willis S. Bird, leg, slight; Wm. J. Bowers, breast, slight; Amos Corns, abdomen, severe, prisoner; Wheeler Chadwick, ankle, severe, prisoner; Benjamin Cruzen, hip, severe, prisoner; Lewis H. Cochran, back, slight; Adam Eichelbarger, thigh, severe, prisoner; James W. Grover, leg, slight, prisoner; John B. Harris, thigh, slight; Anthony Hawk, knee, severe, prisoner; Philander M. Miller, abdomen, slight, prisoner; John H. Miller, leg, severe, prisoner; Samuel S. Robertson, breast, slight; Joseph Redpath, arm, slight; Levi Shaw, head, slight; Daniel Baun, leg, slight.

COMPANY F.—Corp'l S. B. Montgomery, thigh, slightly; Private W. Gibson, leg, severely, prisoner.

COMPANY G.—Corp'ls John K. Fidler, knees, severely, prisoner; Lucien Reynolds, arm, severely, prisoner; Privates William O. Downs, neck, severely; John Henry, leg, severely, prisoner; John Nurmeyer, sr., leg, severely, prisoner; Isaac N. Ritner, thigh, slightly; Jacob Taylor, neck severely, prisoner; George W. Towne, face and thigh, severely, prisoner; Thomas D. Wallace, leg, slightly; Stephanus Dekock, arm, severely.

COMPANY H.—2d Sergt. Philip L. Suiter, shoulder, severely, prisoner; 5th Sergt. John Wightman, abdomen, mortally, prisoner; Corp'ls T. J. Lawler, hand, severely; James Garret, leg, slightly; C. J. Goldthwaite, arm, severely; David Hollaway, leg, severely, prisoner; Privates Hiner Dorman, neck, severely; John Shoff, leg, slightly; William M. Rodman, groin, severely, prisoner; William T. Disor, abdomen, slightly; James D. Compton, ankle, severely, prisoner; Thomas Lantry, thigh, severely, prisoner; William J Parke, neck, mortally, prisoner; M. A. Peck, legs, severely, prisoner; A. A. McNeil, side, severely; William R. Hoyt, hand, slightly; O. P. McNeil, neck, slightly.

COMPANY I.—Sergeants Oscar L. Jones, arm, slightly; Peter K. Bonebrake, shoulder, slightly; Corporal James W. Strong, leg, severely, prisoner; Privates Joseph Brobst, breast, severely, prisoner; Smith Dunlap, leg, severely, prisoner; John M. McClelland, hip, slightly; Eri Goodenough, arm, slightly; Enoch Palmer, head, slightly; William G. Reed, leg, slightly; John S. Snyder, leg, severely, prisoner; James I. Welch, abdomen, severely, prisoner; John Bruett, arm, severely, prisoner.

COMPANY K.—Corporals George B. Stratton, thigh, severely, prisoner; William R. Cowan, leg, slightly; Privates D. T. Evans, head, slightly; E. F. Henderson, back, severely; J. C. Roberts, leg, slightly; John M. Martin, arm, slightly; F. M. Playel, leg, severely, prisoner; William H. Coulburn, leg, severely, prisoner; Samuel Smith, ankle, severely, prisoner; Alexander Jones, head, severely, prisoner; H. C. Haskell, leg, severely, prisoner; Ephriam S. Smith, side, severely, prisoner.

MISSING.—Privates John R. Allsup, Co. B; Francis M. Dyer, Co. B; Clark Boon, Co. H; James Wendell, Co. K; Hannibal Rogers, Co. B; Reuben Coomes, Co. C; F. M. Gibson, Co. F; Kryn De Bruyn, Co. G; John Nurmeyer, jr., Co. G; Hans Ferguson, Co. I; David T. Welch, Co. I; George S. Carson, Co. E, April 23. These men have all since been accounted for. Nathaniel H. Richardson, Co. A, David Dunbar, Co. E, Daniel A. Wisir, Co. G, and Samuel M. Tennis, Co. H, were taken prisoners with train near Mark's Mills, April 23d, 1864.

All the above casualties, except when another time is given, occurred on the 30th of April.

RECAPITULATION.—Killed—enlisted men, 8. Wounded—commissioned officers, 6; enlisted men, 97. Missing, 12. Total, 123.

Lost under Major Gibson, 5; prisoners, 4; entire loss on expedition, 133.

PARTIAL HISTORY OF THE REGIMENT.

HEAD-QUARTERS 33D IOWA INFANTY VOLUNTEERS,
MCINTOSH'S BLUFF, ALA., May 1, 1865.

GEN. N. B. BAKER, *Adjutant-General of Iowa:*

GENERAL:—I have the honor to make the following report of operations of the 33d Iowa Infantry from October 30, 1864. We left Little Rock, Ark., to escort a supply train of two hundred wagons to Fort Smith, Ark., a distance of 180 miles. We marched to Fort Smith, and returned with the train in twenty-nine days. Number of days marched, twenty-six; entire distance traveled three hundred and sixty miles, all of which was accomplished without the loss of a single team or soldier. This march was made at the time of Gen. Price's retreat from Missouri, and we captured two officers and thirty-eight men belonging to his command.

On the 21st day of January, 1865, the regiment started on an expedition from Little Rock to Mt. Elba, Ark., on the Saline river, and returned on the 4th day of February, 1865, to Little Rock. Distance traveled one hundred and sixty miles.

On our return to Little Rock we were ordered to report to Major-General Canby at New Orleans.

Left Little Rock for New Orleans on the 14th day of February, 1865, and arrived at the latter place, February 19th, 1865. From Little Rock to Duvall's Bluffs, we were transported by railroad; from the latter place to New Orleans, by steamboat. On the 23d day of February, 1865, we left New Orleans on Ponchartrain Railroad, and from the terminus of this road—Lakeport—took transports for Navy Cove, Ala. It was at this place that the army was organized for the expedition against the city of Mobile. By this organization we were transferred from the 7th Army Corps to the 13th.

On the 17th day of March, 1865, the movement against Mobile commenced, the 13th Army Corps moving by land around Mobile Bay, east side. The country through which we moved is generally known among citizens as "The Wilderness." We were compelled to make miles of corduroy in order to get our trains and artillery through. The distance through "The Wilderness" (we considered ourselves through when we crossed Fish river) is forty-five miles; time occupied seven days. The 16th Army Corps arrived at the mouth of Fish river one day in advance of the 13th. On the 25th day of March, 1865, the two army corps took up their line of march for Spanish Fort, twenty-five miles north of the mouth of Fish river, and nearly opposite the city of Mobile, where we arrived on the evening of the 27th of March, 1865. The enemy's works were completely invested the following morning. On the night of the 8th of April, 1865, the enemy evacuated the place, leaving all their artillery and munitions of war. They evacuated by water, the navy having been unable to cut off this way of retreat.

I append herewith a list of the casualties of the regiment during the siege. The little damage we sustained from the enemy's fire is accounted for in this way: During the first night after we invested the place, we succeeded in pushing our skirmishers so close to the enemy's works that their gunners and sharpshooters could not do us much damage. The gunners could not work their guns, and the sharpshooters of the enemy were compelled to keep inside the main works. On the 9th of April, 1865, we left Spanish Fort for Blakely, twelve miles north, which place had been invested by a portion of our forces under command of Major-General Steele. We arrived there in the evening, just as the place had been carried by assault. We lay at this place until 6 o'clock P. M., April 11th, when we were ordered to retrace our steps to Stark's Landing, (near Spanish Fort,) where we arrived at 4 o'clock the following morning, and immediately embarked on transports and crossed to the opposite side of the bay. That evening we arrived in Mobile, the rebels having evacuated the place.

The following day our division (the 3d) marched from the city of Mobile to Whistler Station, twelve miles; had a slight skirmish with the enemy, and captured a considerable amount of rolling stock of the Mobile & Ohio Railroad.

On the 19th day of April, 1865, we left that place and marched to our present camp, forty miles.

During this campaign we were allowed one six-mule team for every two hundred and fifty men. The men carried in their knapsacks a complete change of underclothing, an extra pair of shoes, one blanket, one poncho, and one shelter tent to every two men, fifty rounds of amunition each, one spade and one ax to every twelve men, and rations were issued every five days. The average number of men for duty in the regiment during the campaign was five hundred and fifty. The health of the command has been very good during the campaign.

I have the honor to be, Colonel, your obedient servant,

C. H. MACKEY, Colonel commanding.

MAY 1st, 1865.

LIST OF CASUALTIES *(all wounded) in Thirty-Third Iowa Infantry Volunteers during the Siege of Spanish Fort, Ala.:*

Wm. S. Parmley,	Captain	Co. B,	breast slightly.
George L. Ledyard,	"	" G,	face, "
Abraham Day,	Corporal,	" F,	foot, "
Wm. Dingeman,	Private,	" G,	face, "
Martin Walraven,	"	" G,	right arm, severely.
John Metz.	"	"	left shoulder, "
Joseph Dungan,	"	" G,	right hip, "
G. W. Long,	"	" B,	right leg, slightly.
Wm. Campbell,	1st Serg't,	" C,	head, "
Thos. J. Gooden,	Private,	" C,	right eye, "
William Harris,	"	" H,	head, mortally.
Stephen Wharton,	"	" E,	mouth, severely.

Respectfully submitted,

C. H. MACKEY, Col. 33d Iowa Infantry.

CONCLUSION OF HISTORY OF REGIMENT.

HEAD-QUARTERS 33D REGIMENT IOWA VOL. INFT.,
DAVENPORT, IOWA, Aug. 8th, 1865.

N. B. Baker, Adjutant General of Iowa:

GENERAL: I have the honor to make the following report of the movement of my regiment since last report, which left me on McIntosh's Bluff

Alabama. On the 1st of June, we received orders to embark on the ocean steamer Continental, for Brazos Santiago, Texas; which order we obeyed, and landed on the Brazos Island on the 7th of July. Remained on the sland one week, during which time we were badly supplied with water, the condenser on the island not being able to furnish sufficient water for the number of the troops there. After remaining here one week, we moved on to the Rio Grande opposite the town of Bagdad.

Here we remained until the 26th of July, when we received orders from Major-General Steele to report to Galveston, Texas, for muster-out of the service. We embarked on the steamer Warrior, on the 1st of July, and arrived at Galveston on the 3d, reporting at that place to Major-General Granger, who ordered us to proceed to New Orleans, La., to make out our rolls for muster-out. Left Galveston on the morning of the 4th of July, and arrived at New Orleans on the 7th, reporting to Major-General Sheridan, who transferred us from the 13th Corps to General Canby's command. We proceeded immediately to making out our rolls and completed them on the 17th of July, and on the 18th started for Davenport. Very poor boats were furnished us to come up the river on, by reason of which we did not arrive in Davenport until the 1st of August. The regiment is being paid off to-day, August 8, 1865.

The health of the command has been good. The three-years recruits of my regiment were not mustered out with the old soldiers, but were transferred to the 34th Iowa. I wish to call your attention to the fact, that nearly all the other regiments are allowed to muster out their recruits. Justice to these men of my regiment, requires that they should be mustered out also. There is no excuse for keeping a few, and allowing the most of them to be mustered out.

The number of enlisted men mustered out, is 400; officers, 30. Total, 430.

I have the honor to be, General, your obedient servant,

C. H. MACKEY, Col. commanding regiment.

THE END